T0312305

Cambridge Elements ≡

Elements in Child Development
edited by
Marc H. Bornstein
National Institute of Child Health and Human Development, Bethesda
Institute for Fiscal Studies, London
UNICEF, New York City

EQUITY FOR CHILDREN IN THE UNITED STATES

Shantel Meek
Arizona State University

Xigrid Soto-Boykin
Arizona State University

Darielle Blevins
Arizona State University

Evandra Catherine
Arizona State University

CAMBRIDGE
UNIVERSITY PRESS

Shaftesbury Road, Cambridge CB2 8EA, United Kingdom

One Liberty Plaza, 20th Floor, New York, NY 10006, USA

477 Williamstown Road, Port Melbourne, VIC 3207, Australia

314–321, 3rd Floor, Plot 3, Splendor Forum, Jasola District Centre, New Delhi – 110025, India

103 Penang Road, #05–06/07, Visioncrest Commercial, Singapore 238467

Cambridge University Press is part of Cambridge University Press & Assessment, a department of the University of Cambridge.

We share the University's mission to contribute to society through the pursuit of education, learning and research at the highest international levels of excellence.

www.cambridge.org
Information on this title: www.cambridge.org/9781009475938

DOI: 10.1017/9781009379755

First published 2024

A catalogue record for this publication is available from the British Library.

ISBN 978-1-009-47593-8 Hardback
ISBN 978-1-009-37972-4 Paperback
ISSN 2632-9948 (online)
ISSN 2632-993X (print)

Cambridge University Press & Assessment has no responsibility for the persistence or accuracy of URLs for external or third-party internet websites referred to in this publication and does not guarantee that any content on such websites is, or will remain, accurate or appropriate.

Equity for Children in the United States

Elements in Child Development

DOI: 10.1017/9781009379755
First published online: April 2024

Shantel Meek
Arizona State University

Xigrid Soto-Boykin
Arizona State University

Darielle Blevins
Arizona State University

Evandra Catherine
Arizona State University

Author for correspondence: Shantel Meek, Shantel.meek@asu.edu

Abstract: All children deserve access to the conditions and opportunities needed to thrive, including unbiased accessible healthcare and high-quality learning opportunities; safe, toxin-free communities and stable housing; access to nutritious meals; and secure, warm, available, and loving caregivers. Historic and contemporary injustices in US society have created inequities in opportunity and access to resources for Black, Latine, Asian, American Indian and Alaska Native, and other children of color, children with disabilities, children in poverty, and other marginalized children; these have contributed to stark disparities across child development outcomes. This Element overviews inequities in economic, educational, and health systems through historical and contemporary perspectives and describes how these inequities impact children and families. Solutions to address these inequities are considered for a fairer US society, starting with its youngest residents, where all families have what they need to thrive. This title is also available as Open Access on Cambridge Core.

This Element also has a video abstract: www.cambridge.org/Meek

Keywords: equity, children, education, health, economic well-being

ISBNs: 9781009475938 (HB), 9781009379724 (PB), 9781009379755 (OC)
ISSNs: 2632-9948 (online), 2632-993X (print)

Contents

1 Introduction

"Equal opportunity for all" has been a stated cornerstone of US American democracy since the founding of the country. These ideals were, of course, not realized at the time, considering many of the men who wrote those ideals legally owned fellow human beings, and the system of slavery, more broadly, was foundational to much of the wealth generated in the new nation. American Indian/Alaskan Native (AI/AN) people, who had inhabited this land first and for generations, were murdered, forced from their land, and prevented from accessing basic resources. Other people of color over the course of US history, as well as disabled[1] individuals, have been marginalized, excluded, and exploited in different ways. Indeed, US American systems – then and now – have not embodied their stated ideals to create the conditions under which all people have equal opportunity to thrive. It has been more than 150 years since the Emancipation Proclamation, and many decades since the Civil Rights Movement established legal precedents and resulted in legislative victories for Black and other communities of color. Still, at this writing in 2023, demographic characteristics are too often predictive of one's outcomes – education, health, wealth, economic, and more.

Throughout this history, children have been the youngest victims of racism, ableism, poverty, and other forms of oppression. Clearly and consistently, data indicate that children from historically marginalized communities, including Black, Latine,[2] AI/AN, and Asian American and Pacific Islander children, children with disabilities, and children living in poverty, have less access to the resources and conditions that foster positive development. Although families of color and their children have immense cultural, linguistic, and community assets (Yosso, 2005), they are more likely to experience daily and lifelong hardships and stressors, stemming from policies and resulting in conditions that have systematically disadvantaged, disenfranchised, and discriminated against people of color in the United States. Factors ranging from a lack of access to affordable housing, quality education, financial capital, and health care, to mass incarceration and deportations, take their toll on families and have for generations. An understanding of children's equity requires a foundational understanding of how the US American systems have been active and/or passive in

---

[1] Disabled is used instead of "people with disabilities" to align with a social model of disability, which acknowledges that ableism and other barriers in society are what is disabling for individuals and that neurodivergent people should not have to change who they are to fit a nondisabled societal mold.

[2] Latine is the gender-neutral term in Spanish for people who were born in or descendants from Latin America.

creating, perpetuating, and entrenching disparities across multiple domains – education, health, wealth generation, economic stability, and so on.

The historical marginalization of people of color was codified in law in order to hoard economic advantage for White people, especially wealthy White men. United States chattel slavery was established for economic purposes and the concept of race and White supremacy were established as justification for the existence of this grotesque inhuman system. White supremacy, built on other human classification systems, such as patriarchy and classism, was one of the nation's earliest attempts to categorize human beings on a hierarchy. This hierarchy was based on the new, invented, nonscientific concept of "race." Over time, White supremacy and the concept of a human hierarchy paved the way for other social variables (disability, sexual orientation, immigration status, ethnicity, and so on) that would determine where people were placed on the hierarchy, and the relative advantage (or disadvantage) and freedom they could enjoy.

Marginalization, contemporarily and historically, has taken and continues to take different forms, including violence, and various levels of legal or de facto exploitation, explicit exclusion from education, health, and economic systems, among others, inequitable resource distribution, inequitable access to social programs and services, and biased treatment within systems. The differences in *access to* and *experiences* in the US American systems today are compounded by historical exclusion and marginalization and still contribute to disparities in *outcomes* between historically marginalized groups and their more advantaged counterparts.

This Element takes a historical and contemporary, intersectional racially conscious approach to understanding children's equity in the United States and reviews research on existing inequities in opportunity and disparities in outcomes that are too common in the lives of young children. We frame this work with an understanding that equity for children necessarily requires equity for families. As such, we begin with a discussion of family economic well-being, considering the central role it plays in children's access to basic needs – safe and stable housing, food security, safe communities, and available, responsive caregivers. Next, we explore access to high-quality, unbiased education, including early education, and access to high-quality health care, including mental health care and nutritious food. We examine existing inequities in access to resources and experiences within the systems that are meant to support children's learning and health, including where and how policies have helped advance equity for children and where they have fallen short.

1.1 What Is Equity for Children?

Children need a consistent, warm, responsive caregiver to thrive. They also need access to health care, safe and stable housing, nutritious food, safe communities, and quality education, including early education. Throughout US American history, this set of conditions has not been a reality for many children and, as a matter of policy or practice, was withheld in different ways, creating historical, continuous, and compounding marginalization for particular groups of children, including Black, AI/AN, and Latine children and other children of color, disabled children, immigrant children, children who speak languages other than English, and children experiencing poverty. Equity for children requires policies, investments, and supports that ensure that all children have access to the resources, relationships, and conditions they need to thrive. It requires providing resources to repair past harms to communities that have been historically marginalized and engaging in specific policy actions that address inequities in both *access* to systems and *experiences* within systems, with a key goal of closing opportunity gaps and disparities in *outcomes* across social demographic groups. Equity requires an understanding of and explicit attention to historical inequities, their roots, and their evolution over time in order to establish policies and practices that will advance equitable opportunity and close disparities.

1.2 Theoretical Frameworks for Understanding Equity for Children and Their Families

Traditionally, when examining how children fare in our education, health, and other systems, a number of prevalent theoretical framings focus on the role of individual factors (e.g., parenting, child academic skills, children's perceived deficits) on children's and families' outcomes (e.g., Hart & Risley, 1995). In education, for example, prominent theoretical framings that focus on individuals, rather than systems, include the "achievement gap" (e.g., Coleman, 1969) and the "word gap" (e.g., Hart & Risley, 1995). According to the "achievement gap," which was first conceptualized by James Coleman in 1969, a combination of home, community, and school factors create academic outcomes for children. Similarly, researchers who subscribe to the "word gap" postulate that families from low-income backgrounds speak less to their children than those from middle-income families; therefore, by the age of three, children from low-income backgrounds are exposed to thirty million fewer words than children whose families are from middle-incomes and higher (e.g., Greenwood et al., 2020; Hart & Risley, 1995; Logan et al., 2019; Walker & Carta, 2020). Like the achievement gap, this word gap has been conceptualized as a public health concern and attributed to resulting in poor educational, economic, and social outcomes (e.g., Greenwood et al., 2017). Both the achievement and word gaps spurred the development of nationwide policy agendas and research initiatives (e.g., Bridging the Word Gap Research Network). However, over the last couple of decades, a number of scholars, particularly Black and other scholars of color, have problematized theoretical framings such as the "achievement gap" and "word gap" because they are color-evasive and because they do not consider the societal context in which families and children live, especially the impact of historic and contemporary racism and advantage (e.g., Cushing, 2022; Gardner-Neblett et al., 2023; Kuchirko, 2019). Garnder-Neblett and colleagues (2023), for example, note that the achievement gap is problematic because without interrogating the impact of racism, it sets White children as the standard, elevates Eurocentric norms as the default, ignores the flaws of standardized assessments, and reinforces negative ideologies about Black children's educational underperformance. In other words, theories that focus on individuals miss the sociopolitical contexts impacting the health, education, and economic outcomes of Black, Latine, Indigenous, and other children and families of color.

There is too often little mention of the systemic inequities impacting the conditions under which children and families live, which in turn impact access to opportunity and ultimately a range of developmental and academic outcomes. A narrow focus on addressing gaps in children's test scores, for example, fails to take into account children's access to well-funded schools, nutritious meals, or safe and stable housing. It does not take into account exposure to racism, unsafe communities, and high levels of stress associated with financial instability. All of these factors greatly impact children's opportunities to regularly attend and thrive in school as well as parents' bandwidth and time to support their children's development. Children living in low-income households and children of color are often the focus of research aiming to close achievement gaps or perceived gaps in parenting behavior, and the underlying ideologies suggest that these children and families, in particular, need to be "fixed," without attending to historical and contemporary inequitable access to resources and opportunity, and the burdens of stress due to poverty, racism, and other oppressions that these families have faced and continue to face.

System-focused, intersectional ecological model on children's equity. Iruka and colleagues (2022) build on previous ecologically focused theories (e.g., Coll et al., 1996) to conceptualize the *Racism + Resilience + Resistance Integrative Study of Childhood Ecosystem* (R³ISE, Figure 1) framework. According to R³ISE, there are four types of racism that impact Black, Latine, and other individuals of color intergenerationally prenatally to old age, as well as family and community assets that moderate the impact of these four types of racism.

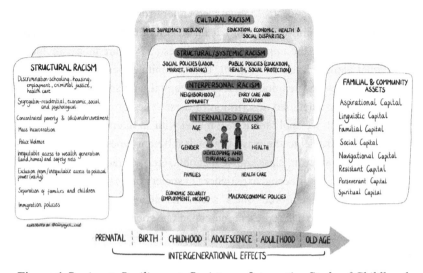

Figure 1 *Racism + Resilience + Resistance Integrative Study of Childhood Ecosystem* (R³ISE, Iruka et al., 2022)

Note. This figure is being reprinted with permission from the authors. Original sources are: Iruka, I. U., Gardner-Neblett, N., Telfer, N. A., Ibekwe-Okafor, N., Curenton, S. M., Sims, J., ... & Neblett, E. W. (2022). Effects of racism on child development: Advancing antiracist developmental science. *Annual Review of Developmental Psychology, 4,* 109–132; Iruka, I. U, Clepper-Faith, M., & Forte, A. (2023), *Advancing Racial Equity in Child Development through Antiracist Developmental Science.* Equity Research Action Coalition. https://equity-coalition.fpg.unc.edu/resource/advancing-racial-equity-in-child-development-through-anti racist-developmental-science/.

The combination of these types of racism, and how they are moderated by family and community assets, affect children's healthy development. The four types of racism, organized from broader to more granular racism, include cultural, structural/systemic, interpersonal, and internalized racism. Cultural racism includes ideologies that center Whiteness as superior and the default of what is considered appropriate, "normal," and desirable. Structural/systemic racism includes the social, public, economic, and macro-economic policies that impact individuals. Examples of structural/systemic racism include discrimination in schooling, housing, employment, and the criminal justice system; economic and social segregation; concentrated areas of poverty; mass incarceration; public violence; and inequitable access to generational wealth. Interpersonal racism includes the bias and racism people experience in their neighborhoods and communities, schools, families, and health care. Last but not least, internalized racism is the negative belief that Black and other individuals have about themselves based on their age, gender, and health. The R³ISE model also undergirds that Black, Latine, and other children and families of color have a wealth of familial and community assets that moderate the impact of racism. These assets are many, including aspirational capital, linguistic capital, family capital, social capital, navigational capital, resistant capital, perseverant capital, and spiritual capital (see Yosso (2005) for a detailed description of these types of capital).

In this Element, we apply the R³ISE model with an intersectional approach. Intersectionality refers to the ways in which different types of discrimination (racism, sexism, ableism, classism, xenophobia, etc.) interact with one another to create specific, multifaceted experiences in society that can either exacerbate marginalization or reinforce one's social advantages (Crenshaw, 2013). Children and families can represent more than one social group that is marginalized in society (e.g., by race, gender, disability, immigration status) and have unique, layered experiences of discrimination. For example, a Black Haitian child who is an immigrant and has an intellectual disability may face bias and discrimination in many, compounding ways. The child's immigrant status may make their family ineligible to receive social support, such as food or housing assistance. The child's racial identity may lead teachers to have differential and less favorable perceptions of the child's behavior, potentially putting the child at higher risk for suspension. The child's disability may make it less likely for the child to receive services in a general education setting, which research demonstrates has important benefits (Fisher et al., 2002). The child may be overlooked for bilingual education because of inaccurate depictions of immigrants as Latine and the assumption that all people who are Black are from the United States and speak English (Cioè-Peña, 2017). These assumptions can result in the lack of targeted support (language development, assessment, and translation services) for the child and their family.

The R³ISE model (Iruka et al., 2022), combined with an intersectional framing (Crenshaw, 2013), offers a comprehensive way of understanding the role race and other identities such as gender, income, home language, and disability have on children's access to, experiences with, and outcomes in America's economic, health, and education systems. It also highlights how the strengths of children, families, and communities sustain, protect, and nourish children's healthy development. In this Element, we interweave the realities of racism and other forms of oppression with children and families' assets to better understand how Black, Latine, Indigenous, and other children of color, as well as those with disabilities, are faring – and what can be done to leverage their strengths to optimize their learning and overall well-being.

1.3 Key Concepts Related to Equity

In addition to having a theoretical framework that grounds one's understanding of equity in US economic, education, and health systems, it is also important to have a shared understanding of the equity concepts related to these topics. Today, words related to equity, such as "bias," "diversity," and "inclusion," are commonplace, but individuals, organizations, and governments have different definitions of these words. It is vital to accurately define key concepts related to equity. Table 1 provides an overview of these key concepts.

Table 1 Key concepts related to equity in US economic, education, and health systems

Key concept	Definition
Equity	Equity is the creation of policies and systems in which children and families from historically and contemporary marginalized communities receive greater access to resources to repair past harms, including high-quality services in the education, health, and other systems; have fair and positive experiences within those systems; and experience outcomes that are not associated with their demographic characteristics such as race and ethnicity, language, income, geographic setting, ability, gender, and so on. Equitable distribution of resources and positive experiences within systems consider and account for historical context and the compounding nature of cross-generational marginalization, exclusion, and violence. Every individual and group of people will be valued and all disparities will be eliminated, once equity is achieved.
Race	According to the Human Genome Project, race is not biologically based, meaning that people in different racial categories are not genetically different. Race is a social construct developed to categorize people into a hierarchy, most pervasively by phenotypes, skin color, hair texture, and so on, to hoard and consolidate resources, wealth, and advantage.
Racism	Racism is the historic and modern system of laws, policies, and beliefs that maintain differential access to resources and outcomes based on a person's racial categorization. Racism is present at systemic and personal levels. Systematically, racism exists in US educational, health, economic, and other institutions.

Table 1 (cont.)

Key concept	Definition
	Personally, racism is evident in interpersonal relationships and the negative beliefs, assumptions, and actions one engages in about people of color.
Bias	Bias refers to the beliefs, attitudes, and stereotypes that one has about other people based on lived experiences, values, education, who we interact with, and so on. Bias impacts actions and emotional responses to others, and it can be explicit or implicit.
Implicit and explicit bias	Implicit biases are, automatic, uncontrolled, and unconscious cognitive reactions that impact our actions and attitudes toward people (Iruka et al., 2020). Implicit bias can lead to either favorable or unfavorable characterizations of people. Explicit bias refers to *conscious* beliefs and stereotypes that can influence one's understanding, actions, and decisions (Daumeyer et al., 2019).
Ableism	Ableism refers to the way in which society designs systems and structures centered on people without disabilities and excludes those with disabilities through policies, practices, and perceptions.
Color evasiveness	Color evasiveness is ignoring differences that exist among people and saying things like, "I don't see color," or explaining societal inequities without explicitly addressing the impact of racism. Color evasive approaches are often associated with kindness, but they are harmful because they minimize the impact of racism. In this Element, we intentionally avoid saying "color blindness," as this term has ableist roots.
Intersectionality	Intersectionality refers to the manner in which people's many different identities, such as gender, race, ethnicity, language, ability, income, education, immigration status, and so on, result in various levels of compounded marginalization, or advantage, across various systems and structures in society.
Antibias/ antiracism	Antibias means one is intentionally implementing actions to reduce one's bias and negative assumptions and actions toward other people. Antiracism means one explicitly engages in actions to concretely reduce and dismantle the roots and effects of racism within one's spheres of influence (Kendi, 2022).

2 Equity in Family Economic Wellness

It is impossible to discuss equity for children without discussing equity for families and communities, and equity for families and communities begins with economic wellness – including economic stability, economic mobility, and wealth generation. Equity for families requires an understanding of historical and contemporary exclusion and marginalization of Black, Latine, AI/AN, and other families of color in US American systems, especially economic and financial systems, and necessitates action toward building wellness and opportunity specifically for those families. *Economic stability* is the ability to meet an array of basic needs – food, shelter, health care, and so on (Butrica & Martincheck, 2020); *economic mobility* is change in income over time, whether individually over the course of a person's life (i.e., *intergenerational* economic mobility) or across generations, that is, comparing children to their parents and so on (i.e., *inter*generational economic mobility) (Butler et al., 2008); and *wealth* is the value of assets (e.g., a home) minus debt (e.g., mortgage), which, over time, can provide economic security and opportunity for future generations (Horowitz et al., 2020).

Poverty is inextricably linked to racism, historically and contemporarily. From the period of enslavement and the colonization of land first inhabited by American Indians, resources have been extracted and distributed according to established social racial hierarchies. This extraction and distribution of resources drives racial disparities across an array of outcomes in young children and their families (Heard-Garris et al., 2021), beginning with economic well-being but extending to health, education, and other domains. Today, poverty is pervasive in the United States. In 2020, the US national poverty rate was 11.4% and the child poverty rate was 16%, but rates varied substantially by racial group. Just over 8% of White children, nearly 21% of Latine children, and nearly 27% of Black children lived in poverty (US Census Bureau, 2022a, 2022b). Children growing up in poverty are more likely to face an array of adverse experiences, including material hardship, food insecurity, housing instability, maltreatment, and poor-quality education. Living in poverty is associated with mental health challenges, physical health impairments, lower academic attainment, employment and economic instability in adulthood (National Academies of Sciences, Engineering, and Medicine [NAESM], 2019).

Black and Latine US Americans are overrepresented in many lower wage jobs-a continuous trend across US American history that is tied-for Black people, to slavery, sharecropping, Jim Crow laws, and other policies that exploited and excluded Black people from participating in other types of employment, devalued the work disproportionately done by Black people, and disproportionately left those workers with few, if any, labor protections (Carruthers & Wanamaker, 2017).

Latine people are a racially, linguistically, and culturally diverse group (Funk & Lopez, 2022); however, they are disproportionately impacted by harsh immigration policies and negative immigration experiences, reduced economic and educational opportunities, housing and school segregation, and diminished access to social services, which impact their experiences in the United States. Latine people from Puerto Rico are considered US citizens, but those residing in the island cannot vote in presidential elections or have representatives in Congress and therefore continue to be negatively affected by American colonization that began in 1898 and continues today. As a case in point, 45% of Puerto Ricans residing in the island live below the federal poverty line, causing a large influx of people to move to the mainland United States (US Census, 2023). Regardless of country of origin, Latine people are disproportionately represented in low-wage jobs, particularly domestic and agricultural work, which, beyond wages, also influences the extent of coverage from labor protections (Catanzarite, 2000). Immigrants without documentation also suffer from labor exploitation at rates far higher than their peers (Byrd, 2009). There is also a racial and gender pay gap, resulting in women of color earning less for the same work as their peers, with Latinas earning the least compared to their female peers in other racial categories (Richard, 2014). Each of these differences across employment, wages, and labor protections impacts families' economic stability and overall well-being.

Poverty in AI/AN communities is also driven by historical policies and resource extraction and redistribution, stemming from land theft, forced relocation, and assimilation practices manifested through, for example, child removals to AI/AN boarding schools. These policies have consequences resulting in intergenerational trauma and have been compounded by contemporary marginalization, resulting in high unemployment and underinvestment in critical infrastructure (Around Him & Sauyaq Jean Gordon, 2022). All of these consequences affect the conditions in which children develop, including their access to clean water, health care, and high-quality, culturally sustaining early learning opportunities, and they contribute to disparities in outcomes.

Data also indicate that people of color have less upward economic mobility, but higher downward economic mobility than their White peers. One study found that a White child born to parents at the top income levels is about five times as likely to remain there in adulthood, compared to a Black child from a similarly wealthy family, who is as likely to fall to the bottom group as to remain in the top group. Of children who were born in the bottom fifth of the income distribution, over 10% of White children but only 2.5% of Black children make it to the top fifth as adults (Chetty et al., 2020). Indeed, research has found that Black boys have less upward economic mobility than their White peers in 99% of census tracts (Chetty et al., 2020). Inequitably distributed educational and economic opportunities, paired with systemic and individual biases, and compounded by generations of marginalization and exploitation, reinforce stubborn gaps in economic mobility.

Considering these stark contemporary differences in both economic stability and mobility, particularly against the backdrop of historical exploitation by and exclusion from economic systems in the United States, it is not surprising that a large racial wealth gap exists. The racial wealth gap between Black and White families is stark and intergenerational, with 2016 estimates indicating that the net worth of a typical White family is nearly ten times greater than that of a Black family (Derenoncourt et al., 2022; McIntosh et al., 2017). Because wealth accumulates and appreciates over time, the racial wealth gap is perhaps the clearest manifestation of history's influence on an array of current disparities across groups, starting with slavery, and later, sharecropping and Jim Crow laws, including residential and educational segregation, the refusal to issue loans to Black citizens, the undervaluing of Black property, redlining, and the systematic exclusion of many, disproportionately Black US Americans from worker protections and social security.

The intersection of race and gender also plays an important role in family economic well-being. A well-documented gender pay gap exists that is further compounded by racism, with White women earning 79 cents to every dollar a White man earns, and Black, AI/AN, and Latine women earning 63 cents, 60 cents, and 58 cents, respectively, for every dollar a White man earns (Government Accountability Office, 2022). These wage differences cost women hundreds of thousands of dollars over a lifetime and have significant implications on their and their children's economic well-being. Women's earnings significantly drop, compared to their male counterparts, after the birth of their first child (Kleven et al., 2019), suggesting the presence of a childbearing pay penalty and pointing to important implications for family economic well-being and child poverty.

It is important to note that even when Black Americans and other people of color in the United States reach important economic benchmarks, like home-ownership or college completion, the benefits are often reduced compared to their White counterparts. For example, one analysis found that Black workers with a college degree earn significantly less than their White counterparts with degrees, and only slightly more than White people without degrees (Perry et al., 2021). In fact, data indicate that the size of the racial wage gap actually increased in higher levels of education (Geary, 2022). Black, Latine, Asian, and AI/AN people are less likely to be approved for home loans and become homeowners in the first place. For Black individuals, in particular, the Black–White gap in loan approvals, again, grew larger as income levels increased (Glantz & Martinez, 2018). For those who do attain home ownership, data indicate that Black and Latine individuals are nearly twice as likely as White individuals to receive low appraisals (Freddie Mac, 2022).

Despite historic and contemporary racial inequities in the US economic system, in many communities of color, economic well-being is enabled by strategies rooted in collectivism, which places the group's needs and goals above those of the individual. For example, certain Asian and Latine families combine their financial resources by residing in multigenerational households and sharing assets such as vehicles. Entrepreneurship can be a beneficial means for various groups to generate financial resources and support their communities. Take, for instance, numerous Black entrepreneurs who establish businesses that cater to their community's interests, create employment opportunities and generate income for their community. In return, community members support these Black-owned businesses, fostering a sense of unity and growth within the community (Bates, 2006). This is not unique to the Black community; the number of Latine-owned businesses grew by 8% from 2019 to 2020 (Census Bureau, 2021). Indeed, these practices have economic benefits; they also enable members of groups who experience discrimination in primarily White spaces to enjoy the psychological safety of communing with people who share their lived experiences.

Various public programs and policies have been enacted to address economic stability in particular subgroups of US Americans, such as Social Security (for the elderly), Temporary Assistance for Needy Families (TANF) (for low-income people), and the Child Tax Credit (CTC) (for people with children). The CTC has proven an especially effective intervention at combating child poverty and promoting family well-being. The US American Rescue Plan Act expanded access to and increased the value of the CTC, decreasing child poverty by an estimated 40%. Over 90% of families with low incomes used their tax credit for basic needs, like food and rent (Zippel, 2021). The temporary expansion of the CTC ended in December 2021, resulting in nearly four million children falling back into poverty (Center for Poverty & Social Action, 2022).

2.1 Conclusion

Family economic well-being helps to shape children's home environment, influences children's access to basic needs, is associated with children's health and educational outcomes, and sets the stage for economic mobility in future generations (NASM, 2019). In understanding families' economic wellness, it is critical to understand where disparities in economic wellness began in US history and how those disparities were reinforced over the centuries through policy and practice. Through this historical lens, researchers, administrators, and policymakers can better understand the intersections between racism and poverty and their dual and intersectional impact on children's experiences, opportunities, and outcomes.

3 Equity in Children's Learning and Education

Equity in learning and education systems includes access to well resourced, quality education, learning, and care. It also means that children and their families have experiences within the education system that are nurturing, culturally responsive-sustaining, and antibias/antiracist. When children and their families have access to high-quality, positive educational experiences, they are more likely to have academic and social outcomes that are not predicted by or associated with sociodemographic factors such as their race and ethnicity, income, language, and ability.

3.1 Equity in Education

Children need access to high-quality learning opportunities across their developmental trajectories, starting with early childhood. These must include well-resourced schools and early childhood programs; safe, healthy, and engaging physical facilities; effective, engaging instruction and developmentally appropriate, culturally responsive-sustaining pedagogy; well prepared, supported, and compensated educators; and a positive learning environment and school climate that partners with families and embraces children's cultures and languages. It must include holistic support (e.g., access to community resources, counseling, etc.) for children and their families, including health and mental health supports. All of this must coexist with an intentional awareness and concrete policies and actions that combat bias and racism in all their forms; full inclusion, support, and appropriate accommodations for children with disabilities; and targeted, culturally and linguistically sustaining support for dual language learners (DLLs) with opportunities to foster and grow their bi/multilingualism.

3.2 Historical Context in Education Systems

Access to high-quality learning and education systems, starting in the earliest years and continuing across the educational trajectory, is critical across a range of long-term outcomes, including employment and earnings, well-being, health, and economic mobility (McCoy et al., 2017). Education has been called "the great equalizer" in US American society (Growe & Montgomery, 2003). But like most other US American systems, in too many instances, it reflects and further entrenches inequities experienced by historically and contemporaneously marginalized children. These inequities in the US education system are not new and have continued, albeit in different forms, since the earliest days of the nation (Nelson & Wiliams, 2019).

During the initial inception of the nation, anti-literacy laws and other slave codes made it illegal for enslaved people to learn, and for any person to teach them to read and write. Despite grave danger in doing so, enslaved Africans resisted, organized, and established creative approaches to come together and learn to read (Willis, 2022). Later in the nation's history, as education systems were being established, non-White and disabled children were denied access, and in many cases, Black communities established their own systems of education. From the 1880s to the 1930s, AI/AN children were forcibly removed from their communities to attend boarding schools. The aim of these boarding schools was to assimilate AI/AN children to White society, requiring them to forego their language, culture, spirituality, food, and family lives, as these were considered "uncivilized" (Kids Matter Inc, 2023). The conditions of these boarding schools were abhorrent, riddled with abuse and resulting in countless deaths (Kids Matter Inc, 2023). Even after these boarding schools closed, in 1978, 25–35% of all AI/AN children were removed from their homes, placed in the child welfare system, and adopted by White families (Kids Matter Inc, 2023). In 1978, the Indian Child Welfare Act was passed to address this issue and protect children from being removed from their families and tribal communities.

Black children and adults have also faced significant restrictions in accessing education. During the period of enslavement, literacy laws made it a crime for Black people to learn to read (Williams, 2009). After emancipation, Black communities were allowed to form education systems, but Jim Crow laws required separate systems for Black and White students, and with this segregation, grossly unequal funding and resources. The purpose of these separate systems, like anti-literacy laws centuries earlier and continuous efforts to deny access to quality educational opportunities in the years in between and since, was to maintain and hoard power, resources, and opportunity in White communities (e.g., Darling-Hammon, 2013).

Still, the resiliency and ingenuity in marginalized communities was clear. Black schools that were segregated were not provided with adequate resources, but they offered Black children the opportunity to receive an education from Black teachers. In the early 1900s, Black educators such as Mary McCloud-Bethune and Anna Julia Cooper developed their own approaches to educating Black children, separate from the White school systems. These philosophies were tailored to meet the needs of Black children and families (Giles, 2006; McCluskey, 1989). After *Brown* v. *Board of Education* between 1952 and 1954, the federal government issued desegregation orders in states across the South and outlawed the formal or explicit exclusion of Black children from historically White education systems. Although these efforts paved the way for critical gains in the civil rights of Black communities, they were incomplete, in most cases solely taking into account the physical placement of Black children into what had been exclusively White schools. In many cases, White parents, teachers, students, and other community members vehemently opposed it, resulting in traumatic experiences for many Black children. Black teachers, leaders, and pedagogy were not similarly integrated. This resulted in incomplete and woefully inadequate integration (Meek et al., 2020). Decades later, even physical integration has backslid due in part to several court decisions that have ended desegregation orders in hundreds of communities, affecting millions of students of color, with Latine students being the most segregated group of students nationally (Frankenberg et al., 2019).

Latine children, and specifically Mexican or Mexican American children, also faced explicit exclusion during this period of segregation. In the Southwest and California, "Mexican schools" were established to educate Mexican or Mexican origin children separately from their White peers (Powers, 2008). "Language" was a primary reason cited for the exclusion of these children, with advocates of segregation pointing to the need for these children to be educated in separate settings so they could learn English. Evidence later showed that children were often placed in these schools based on their last name, with no English assessments even conducted (Hodgson, 2022). A major case regarding school segregation was brought by Mexican American families challenging these separate schools in California in the *Mendez* v. *Westimenter* case in 1946. The families were successful, and the case was one of many that predated and paved the way for *Brown* v. *Board of Education* in the Supreme Court and spurred the Bilingual Education Act of 1968 and other legislature to protect the rights of emergent bilingual children. From these earliest days, language and race were woven together in a concept some scholars refer to as the racialization of language. Indeed, still today, the dominant language in US education systems is English and children are still segregated on the basis of English proficiency, often lacking adequate supports to embrace their strengths and promote their holistic development. Pedagogical approaches, assessment, curricula, and instruction are often inadequate to support these children's development, resulting in inequitable experiences and opportunities in education, and in most localities, low graduation rates, compared to their peers (Castro & Meek, 2022).

Children with disabilities are another group that was historically excluded from receiving an education. Prior to the passing of the Individual with Disabilities Education Act (IDEA), formerly known as the Education for All Handicapped Children Act of 1975, there were no legal safeguards for children with disabilities (Peterson, 2016). As a result, children with disabilities were frequently institutionalized, did not attend school, or attended schools without any individualized support. Spurred by *Brown* v. *Board of Education* and the Civil Rights Movement, disability justice advocates began fighting for children with disabilities to have access to equal education opportunities. In 1972, in *Pennsylvania Association for Retarded Children (PARC)* v. *Commonwealth of Pennsylvania*, members of PARC and families of children with disabilities used the Brown decision to argue that all children with intellectual disabilities between the ages of 6 and 21 years old in Pennsylvania had the right to a free public education. That same year, in the *Mills* v. *Board of Education of the District of Columbia* case, it was ruled that children with behavior, cognitive, physical, and emotional disabilities should also have access to a public education and that a lack of funds could not be used to exclude these children. Subsequently, twenty-seven different courts followed suit after PARC and Mills. Then, in 1975, IDEA was passed. Under IDEA, children between three and twenty-one years old had the right to a free and public education, and infants and toddlers from birth to two years of age had the right to early intervention. This law set the maximum federal share for funding of IDEA at 40% of the per child cost; however, the federal budget has never even approached that figure, and currently only 14.7% of the total cost has been funded (National Center for Learning Disabilities, 2021). IDEA was reauthorized in 2004, and amended in 2015, with the passing of the Every Student Succeeds Act. Section 504 of the Rehabilitation Act of 1973, later evolving to the Americans with Disabilities Act, prohibits discrimination of children with disabilities in public or private schools that receive federal financial support and requires that children with disabilities receive accommodations, even if they do not qualify for IDEA services. Although IDEA and Section 504 offer civil protections for children with disabilities so they can access an education, these federal laws were passed only forty-nine years ago. Only twenty-four years ago, in the *Olmstead* v. *L. C.* case, the Supreme Court ruled that people with disabilities had the right to live in the community rather than institutions. This brief history undergirds the continued need to ensure that the rights of children with disabilities are protected and guaranteed, across systems, including in the education system.

Disability history has a deep intersection with the history of racism in the United States. From the late nineteenth century until the 1940s, eugenics was a prominent pseudoscientific and immoral movement in the United States (National Human Genome Research Institute, 2021). The goal of eugenics was to maintain what was perceived as genetic superiority of White people and was used to justify racist practices, like forced sterilization. The eugenics movement also directly spurred the development of standardized assessments such as the Stanford-Binet Intelligence Scale and the Scholastic Aptitude Test (SAT) – both developed in the 1920s (Rosales & Walker, 2021). These assessments, undergirded by the eugenics movement, directly tie to how children with disabilities, especially those who are Black, are treated today. These standardized assessments were originally used to segregate soldiers by test scores and race during World War I. Today, they have resulted in bias and discrimination toward children of color, dual language learners, children with disabilities, and those living in poverty (Rosales & Walker, 2021). For instance, according to the US Department of Education (2022a), Black boys are disproportionately placed in special education with diagnoses of intellectual disability and emotional disturbances, with the former diagnosis often made based solely on the results of biased standardized assessments and the latter reliant on subjective diagnoses that are also biased. At the time that IDEA was passed, it was common belief that Black and other non-White groups were associated with lack of intelligence and aggressive and angry demeanors (Artiles & Kozleski, 2007; Coutinho et al., 2002). Moreover, findings from a 2019 study by Hasan and Kumar revealed there is a strong correlation between scores on standardized assessments and property values. Schools with higher ratings are in turn more likely to be in communities with higher property values. Furthermore, when *Brown* v. *Board of Education* passed, special education was used to segregate Black children in a more inconspicuous way (Skiba et al., 2002). Together, these findings show that disability, race, income, and other demographic variables are intertwined and that people who are at the intersections of one or more of these identities have experienced, and continue to experience, grave inequities in learning and education systems.

3.3 Current Inequities in Educational Access and Opportunities

Today, the exclusion of children from historically marginalized communities takes different forms (Artiles, 2019; Artiles, Dorn, & Bal, 2016). Inequities in educational opportunities have been persistent for certain groups, especially Black children. This is evidenced by the disproportionate use of suspension and expulsion with Black children (Meek et al., 2020; Meek & Gilliam, 2016), lower access to early intervention and early childhood special education

(US Department of Education, 2023), and limited access to gifted and talented programs (Iruka, 2022). Dual language learners similarly face challenges accessing the bilingual education that research supports is most effective for this population (e.g., Barnett et al., 2007).

Although racial segregation is no longer legal, schools are more racially segregated today than they have been in the last forty years (Frankenberg et al., 2019; Reardon & Owens, 2014), with Latine students, in particular, being the most segregated group (Colón et al., 2022). Black children are consistently – across time, place, and groups – disproportionately suspended and expelled from educational systems starting in early childhood, even though no credible evidence exists pointing to more frequent misbehavior in Black children (Gilliam et al., 2016; Skiba et al., 2002). For instance, Black preschoolers received 2.5 more suspensions than their share of preschool enrollment (Civil Rights Data Collection, 2021). Relative to their proportion of enrollment of children with disabilities, Black and Latine children are underrepresented in early intervention and early childhood special education services (EI/ECSE), yet overrepresented in K–12 settings. For young children with disabilities, EI/ECSE are critical to their developmental trajectory (US Department of Education, 2022a). In K–12, Black, Latine, Asian, and Hawaiian Pacific Islander children are more likely to receive special education services in segregated settings than the national average (US Department of Education, 2022a). Dual language learners and English learners (ELs), a disproportionate number of whom are Latines (59%), are often segregated from their peers for part of the school day or "pulled out" for English instruction, driven in part, by misguided ideology, the lack of bilingual programs available to students, and the under-utilization of "push in" models that support EL children in learning alongside their peers (Gandara & Orfield, 2012; Garver & Hopkins, 2020).

Moreover, research also shows inequities in gifted and talented education (GATE) programs (Flynn, 2023; Ford, 2021; Iruka, 2022). In a longitudinal study of gifted program enrollment using data from the Civil Rights Data Collection (CRDC) between 2011 and 2018, White students were consistently overrepresented in gifted programs compared to their peers (Flynn, 2023). CRDC data show that Black and Latine students represent about 42% of K–12 enrollment, but only 28% of GATE enrollment (US Department of Education, 2020). Research finds that White children are about twice as likely to be in GATE programs, even when factors like math and reading scores are the same (Ford, 2021; Ford et al., 2008; Iruka, 2022). Researchers have identified several potential contributors to these disparities, including how "giftedness" is defined and assessed, the referral process, and placement of GATE programs according to community demographics (Ford, 2021; Ford, Grantham, & Whiting, 2008).

Beyond continued segregated learning for various groups, including those in gifted programs, funding continues to be inequitable, with districts that serve majority students of color, compared to those serving majority White students, receiving 16% less funding, on average, from state and local revenue (The Education Trust, 2022b). Those districts serving the most English learners receive 14% less and high-poverty districts receive 5% less. In some states, some groups of marginalized students are funded at higher levels, while others are not, painting a complex picture of equitable funding in the K–12 education system. Even in states that provide more funding for marginalized groups, the added funding is not enough to offset funding disparities at the local level, resulting in less overall funding in schools that serve children in poverty, English learners, and children of color (Morgan, 2018). Previous research and data have consistently found similar trends in differences in funding (Rothbart, 2020). On virtually every concrete measure – from the number of qualified teachers to the availability of research-based curricula – schools serving primarily minoritized children have fewer resources than those serving primarily White children (e.g., Farkas, 2003; Weathers & Sosina, 2022).

Many of these inequities begin in the early years, before kindergarten. Although decades of research have found that access to high-quality early education is associated with short- and long-term benefits across education, health, employment, and other social outcomes (Goodman & Sianesi, 2005; Shonkoff & Phillips, 2000), access is not universal, differing greatly across state lines and across race, language, income, and citizenship (National Institute for Early Education and Research [NIEER], 2021). This is particularly true for learning experiences that are considered "high quality," encompassing a variety of factors like small group sizes and ratios, qualified teachers, play-based or project-based pedagogies, research-informed instruction, and connections to other critical services for children and families, like health, mental health, and food assistance (Trust for Learning, 2023). Only 3% and 4% of Latine and Black young children, respectively, have access to care that is deemed high quality (Gillespie, 2019). In early childhood, public investments at the state and federal level have attempted to extend greater access to particular groups, most commonly children living in low-income households, through programs such as the federally funded Head Start program, childcare assistance subsidies for working families, or state or locally funded pre-K systems, and for children with disabilities through early intervention and preschool special education services. Still, access to high-quality care remains uneven and inequitable (Ullrich et al., 2019). For example, Head Start and Early Head Start only serve 50% and 12% of eligible children, respectively (Hardy et al., 2020). Only 15% of children eligible for childcare subsidies based on federal rules

actually get support (Office of Child Care, 2020). Only 5% and 29% of three-
and four-year-olds have access to public pre-K, respectively (NIEER, 2021).
What's more, the targeted nature of these funding streams in many cases results
in socioeconomic or disability-based segregation, particularly where states and
local communities do not blend or braid funds across various funding streams
and keep children physically separated by funding stream.

Children with disabilities are too often systematically excluded from inclusive early education programs. Only 44% of preschoolers and 60% of school-
aged children with disabilities receive 80% or more of their special education
services in general education settings (US Department of Education, 2022a).
Despite the clear provision in the Individuals with Disabilities Education Act to
ensure children receive services in the least restrictive environment, and several
efforts by both the US Departments of Education, which oversees the special
education system, and Health and Human Services, which oversees the major
early care and education systems, the percentage of children with disabilities
receiving their services in general early childhood programs, alongside their
peers without disabilities has barely budged in decades (US Department of
Education, 2022a) and notably regressed during the pandemic (US Department
of Education, 2023).

These disproportional differences in children's access and opportunities
within the education system have pervasive and long-lasting consequences.
One primary positive outcome of a robust learning and education system is
the extent to which it prepares children to attend college and gain financial
freedom. Whereas college education is one of the primary vehicles to reducing
poverty and narrowing wealth gaps between people of color and White individuals, diminished access and negative experiences in education result in less
access to a higher education for Black, Latine, AI/AN, and other people of color
as well as those with disabilities (United Negro College Fund, 2023). For
instance, only 57% of Black students have access to college readiness courses,
compared to 81% of Asian American and 71% White students. Only 38% of
students taking Advanced Placement courses are Black and Latine, and those
groups are less likely to be enrolled in gifted programs compared to White
students. Moreover, only 68% of students with specific learning disabilities
graduate with a regular high school diploma, only 18% of college students have
disabilities, and 39.5% of adults with disabilities are unemployed (National
Center for Learning Disabilities, 2013). These stark statistics urge us to envision
and implement an equitable learning and education system capable of serving
all children in the United States, especially those who have and continue to be
excluded and marginalized.

3.4 Creating Positive and Equitable Experiences in Learning and Education Systems

There is no single definition of high-quality programming across age groups, but experts generally agree that the following factors are critical: learning standards and curricula that address the whole child; nurturing child–teacher interactions by educators who are antibias/antiracist; child-centered, developmentally appropriate pedagogy and instruction; assessments that are valid and guide data-based decisions about children's needs, strategic planning, and educators' professional development; a well-qualified and compensated workforce that receives ongoing professional development; holistic family engagement; mental health support for social and emotional development; full inclusion of children with disabilities in general education; bilingual support for dual language learners/English learners; and connections to other critical services for children and families, like health and food assistance, are critical (NIEER, 2021; Trust for Learning, 2023). Additionally, research-supported strategies that are effective for children with disabilities, such as individualized instruction, small groups, and the integration of multiple modalities, are also effective for children without disabilities in learning and developmental outcomes (Capp, 2017). Implementing these research-supported strategies that are hallmarks of quality are most beneficial for children from lower income communities and children who are dual language learners (Wechsler et al., 2016).

Learning and educational experiences, to be considered high quality, must meet the needs of children and families from historically and contemporaneously marginalized communities. High-quality programming requires an understanding and acknowledgment of existing and historic inequities in opportunity and disparities in outcomes, with targeted remedies. It requires strength-based pedagogies that are culturally sustaining, bilingual education for those who are dual language learners/English learners, inclusive education for those with disabilities, and mental health supports to prevent suspensions and expulsions and to promote socioemotional development. Commonly used metrics of quality seldom include indicators that address these issues, which disproportionately affect children from marginalized communities (Meek et al., 2022). However, no learning or educational system should be considered high quality if these children's and their families' experiences are negative or if their experiences are not a mandatory metric of quality.

Children's access to high-quality educational programs lead to a range of positive short- and long-term outcomes, including less need for special education services during the PK–12 years, higher graduation rates, and greater chances of employment (Thompson & Thompson, 2018; Workman & Ullrich, 2017).

Investing in high-quality education, starting in early care and education, has immense short- and long-term benefits (McCoy et al., 2017). For example, economists assert that investing in early childhood generates approximately $7 for each dollar invested (Weschsler et al., 2016). Importantly, these outcomes are entirely dependent on the quality of programming. However, for these investments to be materialized, children need to attend high-quality programming. While quality is variously operationalized, core components of quality include child-centered and research-supported curricula that address the whole child; pedagogy and instruction that are antibias/antiracist; ongoing educator professional development; teachers that are equitably compensated; mental health supports and no harsh discipline; bilingual education for dual language learners; and complete inclusion of children with disabilities. We discuss each dimension next.

Defining features of high-quality education for children of color. Black, Latine, AI/AN, and other children of color and those with disabilities require intentional and targeted support to ensure that they receive a high-quality education. This includes the use of child-centered pedagogies, high-quality teachers, family leadership and engagement, data-based professional development and evidence-informed instruction, and a well-compensated and trained workforce. Children also deserve educational experiences that match their unique needs – including inclusive education for children with disabilities, bilingual education for children who are dual language learners, and mental health support to avoid harsh discipline. All educational experiences should also be rooted in developmentally appropriate, culturally responsive-sustaining practices, where their identities are not only validated but also legitimized and preserved. We describe each dimension of educational quality in Table 2.

Child-centered pedagogies. High-quality educational programs apply child-centered pedagogies (Trust for Learning, 2023). Examples of child-centered pedagogies for early childhood include Montessori, Reggio Emilia, Tools of the Mind, and Waldorf. Montessori and Waldorf also apply for older students up to high school. All of these pedagogical approaches have an underlying theme of allowing children to lead their own learning through self-selected activities that foster their curiosity and learning and activate multiple developmental domains (e.g., cognitive, social, physical, moral). When high-quality child-centered pedagogies are implemented, children and youth engage in ongoing exploration with their minds, hands, and bodies. They also have the opportunity to learn through observation and participation that allows them to use critical thinking to hypothesize, test theories, and solve problems. Learning experiences are also reflective of children's unique interests, and they are organized in a way that facilitates children's learning with their peers. A core component of these child-centered

Table 2 Dimensions of educational quality for children from historically and contemporaneously marginalized communities

Dimensions of a Quality Education

- Child-centered pedagogies
- Comprehensive learning standards
- High-quality teachers who are well compensated and supported
- Data-driven professional development, evidence-informed instruction, and programming using valid assessments
- Small group or class sizes and appropriate ratios for children's developmental stage
- Family leadership and engagement
- Inclusion of children with disabilities
- Bilingual instruction for children who are DLLs/ELs
- Mental health supports to promote social emotional development and prevent suspensions and expulsions
- Developmentally grounded, asset-based pedagogies

pedagogies is the integration of play or project-based learning (Zoch et al., 2017). For young children, this looks like engaging in various forms of play (e.g., solitary, parallel, social, cooperative, physical, constructive, etc.) in ways that disrupt children's bias and stereotypes to support symbolic thinking, peer socialization, and language, physical, and cognitive development (Kinard et al., 2021). For older students in middle school and beyond, this looks like uninterrupted work periods, multiage groupings, and spiral curricula that expose students to interrelated topics over time to afford opportunities to master skills gradually. A longitudinal study by Dohrmann and colleagues (2007) revealed that high school students enrolled in a public Montessori program from preschool to fifth grade had higher math and science scores than those who were not enrolled, when controlling for gender, income, race, and ethnicity. These findings corroborate that value of offering children of color opportunities to learn through child-centered pedagogies.

Asset-focused, equitable pedagogies. Although Montessori and other child-led pedagogies are promising for all children, there are other types of pedagogies that have been conceptualized to center the experiences and identities of children of color. Even with school integration, dominant norms and expectations in schools have been based on White children from mid- to upper middle class (Paris, 2012). Materials and content for instruction lack cultural relevance and omit or deemphasize key historical or contemporary figures that represent children from racialized backgrounds. Moreover, all children are expected to speak in Standardized American English. Standardized American English (SAE) is a variety of English spoken by Whites from middle to upper class (Flores & Rosa, 2015). We say "standardized" rather than "standard" to highlight that there is no one specific, proper way of communicating; however, the English varieties spoken by White individuals hold the most prestige, as they are associated with intelligence and professionalism (Flores & Rosa, 2015). This centering of Whiteness in education settings propagates deficit-based views of Black, Latine, AI/AN, and other children of color, as they are compared to a "norm" that does not align with their backgrounds.

Black scholar-activists, in conjunction with other marginalized researcher-educators, have developed a series of asset-based educational framings (Aronson & Laughter, 2016). Contrary to dominant educational approaches that center Whiteness and are color-evasive, these asset-based framings underscore the strengths that children of color bring to learning environments (Aronson & Laughter, 2016). Their cultural and linguistic backgrounds are used to ignite their interest in learning about topics that are relevant to them. There are a number of asset-based framings of education, and we will review five primary ones: *anti-bias education* (e.g., Derman-Sparks & Edwards, 2010), *antiracist education* (Pitts, 2020; Simmons, 2019), *culturally responsive teaching* (Gay, 2000), *culturally relevant pedagogy* (Ladson-Billings, 1994, 1998, 2014), and *culturally sustaining pedagogy* (Paris, 2012; Paris & Alim, 2017), and *liberatory pedagogy* (Freire, 1970). These frameworks are sometimes used interchangeably, and they are not mutually exclusive, but each has distinct approaches that are important to understand to implement them in valid and effective ways (see Table 3).

The goal of antibias education (Derman-Sparks & Edwards, 2010) is to acknowledge and interrupt the stereotyping and biases found in education settings and to empower children with the skills and language to name and address human differences and injustices. Educators who apply antibias principles are aware of their implicit beliefs about Black, Latine, Indigenous, and other children and families of color, and they strive to reframe these beliefs as more strength-focused ones (Iruka et al., 2020). For example, an early childhood educator implementing antibias principles will do an inventory of the classroom materials, including books, dolls, and environmental print. They will ensure that these classroom materials reflect the children and families in the classroom, and that Black, and other people of color, are not shown in stereotypical ways (e.g., not every Black man or boy is a basketball player). They will also engage children in age-appropriate discussions about differences among people's skin colors or abilities and model what to do when children witness an unfair situation.

Table 3 Overview of asset-focused pedagogies

Pedagogy	Definition	Aim	Primary Focus	Tenets
Antibias education (Derman-Sparks & Edwards, 2010)	An explicit educational approach that strives to end all forms of bias and discrimination	Eliminate racial stereotypes	Educators' assumptions and instructional practices; children's awareness of human differences and empowerment to understand unfairness	– Each child demonstrates self-awareness, confidence. family pride, and positive social identities – Each child expresses comfort and joy with human diversity, appropriate language for human differences, and caring human connections – Each child recognizes unfairness and has the language to describe the unfairness – Each child demonstrates empowerment to act against discrimination

Table 3 (cont.)

Pedagogy	Definition	Aim	Primary Focus	Tenets
Antiracist education (Simmons, 2019)	Pedagogies that intentionally dismantle systems of oppression by telling the truth about societal injustices, and instilling hope, healing, and restoration in ways that center the brilliance of Black, Indigenous, and other children of color	Dismantle systems of oppression	– Educators' ongoing self-reflection and awareness of power structures; explicit naming and undoing of historic and contemporary injustices; centering on the triumph, joys, and resilience of Black individuals and others of color; understanding of how racism interplays with other oppressive systems such as sexism, ableism, homophobia, xenophobia, and so on	– Acknowledge racism and White supremacy – Teach history that is representative of the truth and the lived experiences of people of color – Act when presented with racism
Culturally responsive teaching (Gay, 2000)	Embedding children's diverse identities and experiences to make instruction relatable to them	Cultural representation of each child	Educators' instructional practices	– Have high expectations – Validate children's cultures – Provide comprehensive instruction that is emotionally, politically, and academically engaging

Pedagogy	Goal	Focus	Level of intervention	Key features
Culturally relevant (Ladson-Billings, 1994, 1998, 2014)	Collectively empowering children emotionally, socially, and politically by encouraging them to have consciousness about society	Understanding of differences between community and White mainstream cultures	Children's and educators' attitudes and beliefs	– Offer new ways to look at the world to unveil injustices – Focus on long-term achievement rather than end-of-year tests – Foster cultural competence – Develop sociopolitical consciousness
Culturally sustaining (Paris, 2012)	Sustain, or foster, children's evolving linguistic and cultural identities to enact social change	Preserving one's culture and linguistic practices while providing access to the dominant culture (White middle class who speaks standardized English)	Children's and educators' attitudes and beliefs	– Value children's languages, practices, and ways of being – Schools are accountable to the community – Curriculum is linked to the cultural and linguistic histories of the community – Children's cultural and linguistic practices are sustained while educators provide access to the dominant culture

Table 3 (cont.)

Pedagogy	Definition	Aim	Primary Focus	Tenets
Liberatory pedagogy (Freire, 1970)	Co-creating learning environments in which both teacher and students have equal power, and where students receive the information to free themselves from oppressive systems	Freedom from oppressive systems	– Teachers not holding all the knowledge and controlling how children learn or behave, but rather co-creating a space where children can learn in their own ways, use critical thinking, and take action toward their liberation from oppression	– Co-creation of knowledge – Shifting classroom dynamics that reinforce that the teacher has all the knowledge and authority – Making learning political – Problem-solving to address social injustice and take action toward one's liberation from oppressive systems

Antiracist education (Pitts, 2020; Simmons, 2019) goes a step further by explicitly naming White supremacy and telling the truth about societal injustice to dismantle systems of oppression and foster children's critical consciousness, while also centering the hopes and brilliance of children and families who are Black, Latine, Indigenous, and others of color. Educators who are antiracist are committed to ongoing self-reflection, learning, and unlearning (Simmons, 2019). They do not deter from uncomfortable situations, but rather embed their daily instruction with opportunities to disrupt racism and other forms of oppression, while centering Black joy, Black excellence, Black strength, and Black innovation, and Black culture (Escayg, 2020). They also ensure that their activism is extended beyond their work days and into their personal lives (Simmons, 2019). This antiracist education can start with even young children, as research supports that children as young as four years old already have an understanding of racial hierarchies (e.g., Sullivan et al., 2021). For example, an antiracist early childhood educator can introduce children to the innovation and cultural wealth of Africans before European colonization and exploitation, and disrupt racist ideologies as children engage in play (Kinard et al., 2021). They can also engage children in activism when they see injustices in the classroom or their communities.

Rooting antibias/antiracist education in culture ensures that the lived experiences and cultural assets of Black, Indigenous, Latine, and other individuals of color are made an essential component of the pedagogy. To this end, scholars have conceptualized culturally responsive, culturally relevant, and culturally sustaining pedagogies and practices. We describe each of these pedagogies and practices next.

Gay (2000) developed culturally responsive practices, also known as culturally responsive teaching, to focus on teacher practice. The primary goal of culturally responsive practices is to represent children's cultural backgrounds to help them have a clear understanding of current US society. She defined culturally responsive practices as those in which teachers used children's cultural knowledge, prior experiences, and background knowledge to make instruction more relevant for Black, Latine, AI/AN, and other children of diverse backgrounds. Teachers who are culturally responsive have high expectations for all students; are multidimensional because they integrate children's diverse cultural knowledge and perspectives; validate every child's culture by representing them in classroom materials and lessons; seek to teach the whole child (i.e., emotionally, socially, politically); commit to transforming society through their instruction; and strive to liberate children from oppressive educational practices that discriminate against them.

In contrast to culturally responsive practices that focus exclusively on teacher practices, Ladson-Billings' (1994; 2014) culturally relevant pedagogy focuses on altering teachers' attitudes and dispositions to empower children collectively. Culturally relevant pedagogy has three primary objectives. First, to foster children's learning while not focusing on standardized assessments. Second, to build children's cultural competence, or one's capacity to recognize and honor one's cultural beliefs while having access to a wider culture so they can advance their socioeconomic status and live the lives they want for themselves. Third, to build children's sociocultural consciousness so they can recognize, understand, and critique existing social inequities. The primary differences between culturally responsive and culturally relevant pedagogies are that the former aims to change teacher practices and the latter focus on changing attitudes and dispositions. Despite their differences, both aim to be mechanisms for fostering children's understanding of social inequalities and how to address them.

Undoubtedly, culturally responsive practices and culturally relevant pedagogies have set a foundation for equity-focused education; however, they primarily focus on representation and inclusion of culture, rather than ways to effectively sustain (or protect and leverage) children's cultural and linguistic backgrounds. Paris and colleagues (2012) built on these two approaches to conceptualize culturally sustaining pedagogy. The primary goals of culturally sustaining pedagogy are to represent and to legitimize the linguistic and cultural identities children bring to schools. In this framework, culture is not only constrained to traditional items associated with culture (such as holidays and foods), but rather includes the rapidly changing culture that young people create themselves through peer interactions (Bucholtz et al., 2017). The goal of culturally sustainable pedagogy is to provide children opportunities to foster, rather than assimilate, their identities, while also giving them the tools to thrive outside their own communities (Paris, 2012). In other words, culturally sustaining pedagogies align with US society's pluralistic composition so they reflect the strengths of a diverse, democratic society. To achieve this, educators recognize that culture, language, and identity are intertwined, and all these aspects are dynamic and ever-changing. For example, Latine students who share community with Black students might integrate African American English and hip-hop culture in their language and cultural practices. In practice, culturally sustaining pedagogies look like using hip-hop lyrics written in African American English to study an artist's use of vocabulary and prose to convey experiences with societal injustice and encouraging children to write songs, poems, or videos about their lived experiences using their own linguistic practices, such as African American English, Spanish/English, and the like. This example highlights why, when implementing culturally sustaining pedagogy, educators should not only attempt to sustain traditional aspects of culture and language but also remain open to how these identities are ever-evolving and intersectional.

Research on the effects of culturally sustaining pedagogies is still emerging. However, existing research indicates that implementing culturally relevant sustaining pedagogies leads to greater social and academic gains (Cholewa et al., 2014; Dee & Penner, 2017). Two areas for continued growth when conceptualizing culturally sustaining pedagogies are concretely defining what this looks like in early care and education and including disability as another dimension of identity. When conceptualizing what it means to sustain one's culture and language, we seldom think about disability culture or include communication of disabled individuals. To ensure culturally sustaining peda-gogies address the needs of all marginalized communities, it is important to include non-spoken communication (the use of vocalizations, gestures, visuals, etc.) as well as American Sign Language and other signed languages (e.g., Black Sign Language). We must also think of the nuanced intersections among culture, language, ability, and identity for Black, AI/AN, Asian, Latine, and other children of color who also have disabilities, as these intersections are sorely missing when conceiving what a high-quality education system looks like. To create high-quality, culturally responsive sustaining learning environ-ments, we must continue striving toward ensuring that educational experiences of children and youth foster their brilliance and joy, without trying to change who they are.

Liberatory pedagogy complements culturally responsive sustaining ones by noting that the goal of education should be to humanize individuals and to co-create spaces with students so they can have access to information that frees them from oppressive societal systems (Freire, 1970). Liberatory pedagogy, coined by Paulo Freire in the seminal *The Pedagogy of the Oppressed*, supports that classrooms should be spaces where teachers are not treated as the ones holding all the knowledge, and that children should not be instructed with partial information aimed at upholding systems of oppression. Freire argued that in traditional schooling, children are viewed as empty vessels and teachers as the ones who deposit knowledge into children's brains. Children are expected to memorize and recall information and to exhibit the behaviors that teachers expect. Freire (1970) argued that the knowledge the teachers share is based on societal norms, and because children are not encouraged to use critical thinking, traditional schooling reifies societal oppressions. In contrast, liberatory peda-gogy focuses on co-creating knowledge, decentering teachers as the onus of expertise, and encouraging students to be critical thinkers and political, thereby taking action against the oppression that impacts them. The aims of liberatory pedagogy are to co-create spaces of learning where children can develop a consciousness of freedom, recognize authoritarian tendencies, connect knowledge to power, and take action.

Complementing liberatory pedagogies are educational practices that center on the brilliance and joy of Black, Indigenous, and children of color by removing White educational norms as the default. For example, centering Black joy helps Black children understand that they are not defined solely by their trauma, inequities, or historical injustices inflicted upon their community (Dunn & Love, 2020; Muhammad, 2021, 2022). Black joy cannot be explained by a single description. It is the freedom to express your true self and embrace your authenticity openly. Centering Black joy does not mean ignoring Black pain or suffering but instead acknowledging that Black joy exists in tandem. In conceptualizing Black joy, scholars generally identify Black joy as the sum of the following four elements: Black brilliance; Black innovation; Black agency; and Black beauty (Adams, 2022; Dunn & Love, 2020; Muhammad, 2021, 2022). In education, it may look like asking children what brings them joy or encouraging children to practice literacy using language that is comfortable for them, including African American English "slang" in written and verbal exchanges (Center of Excellence, 2023; Muhammad, 2021, 2022).

Joyful learning is relevant across all subjects and ages, ranging from pre-K to higher education. Education scholars highlight the role of joy in science education (Adams, 2022; Worsley et al., 2021), history and literacy (Muhammad, 2021, 2022), and children's literature (Buchanan et al., 2021). Educators of Black children must create a curriculum that focuses on not only narratives and stories about pain but also joy and brilliance. In her Historically Responsive Literacy Model framework, Goldy Muhammed (2021, 2022) outlines five pursuits of education: (1) identity; (2) skills; (3) intellect; (4) criticality; and (5) joy. Muhammed suggests practical ways educators can facilitate children's pursuit of joy including asking children and educators to consider, "what can we learn from history (particularly Black excellence) to refashion curriculum and instruction today?" This question gives agency back to Black students who often do not have a say in what they learn and do not have opportunities to learn about their own cultural heritage and history. Additionally, students can center joy by reflecting on the type of experiences that elevate their happiness and joy. Centering Black joy is about using the wisdom of Black people to put equity into action by creating safe spaces that are not sources for more racial trauma. Emerging research supports that centering Black joy is not only relevant for teaching but also an outcome measure that can prevent Black teacher burnout (Adams, 2022; Williams, 2022), support mental health consultants (Center of Excellence, 2023), and help educators unlearn ingrained anti-Black stereotypes (Center of Excellence, 2023).

Other types of pedagogies and practices that are explicitly focused on sustaining the positive racial and cultural identities of children who have been historically and contemporarily marginalized include Indigenous and anti-colonial pedagogies. It is important to explore these pedagogies and educational practices as we imagine more equitable and just ways of supporting the academic and socioemotional outcomes of children of color and those with disabilities.

Comprehensive learning standards. In addition to pedagogies that focus on children's own learning and sustain their positive racial and cultural identities, high-quality education programs have comprehensive learning standards and curricula that address the whole child, are developmentally appropriate, embed strategies to support dual language learners and children with disabilities, and are effectively implemented (Weschsler et al., 2016). These standards address all developmental domains, including children's cognitive and socioemotional development. For students in secondary grades, this includes opportunities to apply critical thinking to spur their civic engagement and social advocacy and access to college readiness and Advanced Placement courses (Lin, 2015). These standards are also meant to require the use of developmentally appropriate curricula that emphasize child-directed learning opportunities that are interactive and language-rich. Key components of quality are the application of comprehensive learning standards and the adaptation of curricula, and programs need to implement these standards and curricula with high fidelity to be considered quality and effective.

High-quality teachers. Learning standards and curricula set the tone for delivering high-quality educational programming, but these regulations and standards alone are not sufficient to offer children high-quality services (Workman & Ullrich, 2017). At the heart of quality services for children and youth is the relationship between children and their teachers. In high-quality programs, educators engage children in nurturing, positive interactions that are warm and responsive. Effective, well-trained educators respond to children's needs, have high levels of engagement, foster children's independence, and intentionally create language-rich, stimulating environments that encourage children to apply critical thinking (Mena Araya, 2020). They also have strength-based views of all the children and families they serve, particularly those who are Black, Latine, AI/AN and other children of color, and those with disabilities, and engage in ongoing self-reflection to identify their biases and ways to improve their instruction (Trust for Learning, 2023). They also co-construct knowledge with children, serving as nurturing guides as children explore and engage in learning. Effective teachers also create a sense of community among children and adults in the learning environment, they intentionally acknowledge and leverage each child's individual differences, they tailor instruction to meet each child's needs, and they understand the impact of adverse childhood experiences on children's development and respond accordingly to children who might be impacted by these adverse traumatic experiences.

In addition to adequate compensation, educators require ongoing professional development to hone their skills (Ditcher & LiBetti, 2021; Podgursky & Springer, 2011). Professional development takes different forms, including one-day in-service training, webinars, readings, coaching, and communities of practice. Educators benefit the most from ongoing professional development, particularly coaching and mentoring (Avalos, 2011). A systematic review of the effects of early childhood educators' professional development on educators' instruction, content knowledge, and child outcomes indicated that educators benefit from embedded coaching opportunities and that coaching has a positive impact on children's language and literacy, socioemotional development, and academic skills (Yang et al., 2022). The review also reaffirmed that effective coaching models consist of co-participation between the coach and teacher, ongoing observation and feedback, joint problem solving, and administrative support. Professional development should also be specific to addressing equity and include topics such as bilingualism, disability, racial equity, antibias, and culturally sustaining pedagogies – topics sorely missing from most preservice teacher education programs or continuing education requirements (Wiedeman, 2002). To successfully implement high-quality, child-centered pedagogies, engage in nurturing interactions, and use data to inform their instruction, educators need adequate wages and ongoing learning opportunities.

Data-driven instruction. High-quality education programs apply data to make decisions about how to best support each child's and youth's learning and development, to plan strategically, and to make decisions about needed topics for professional development (Lane et al., 2020). Children and youth are screened and assessed formally and informally throughout the year using measures that are culturally and linguistically valid to determine their current level of performance and to inform how to adapt instruction to accelerate their development (Schildkamp, 2019). As more directed instruction is delivered, continuous assessments are conducted to determine the effectiveness of instruction and to adapt as necessary. These data are also collected to determine programs' areas of strengths and areas for improvement. For example, leaders might review outcome data at the end of the year to determine the areas they need to prioritize the following year. Likewise, this data is used to inform teachers' professional development goals and priorities. For example, in a preschool classroom where about 70% of the children are not meeting benchmarks on phonological awareness, educators' professional development plans might focus on enhancing their early literacy instruction.

Well-compensated, supported workforce. Implementing high-quality programs requires a well-compensated workforce that is well supported. Early educators are notoriously underpaid compared to almost all other sectors and compared to their peers who teach in the K–12 system. Nationally, childcare workers across all settings earned a mean hourly wage just over $13 (Center for the Study of Child Care Employment, 2020; McLean et al., 2021; US Bureau of Labor Statistics, 2021). A pay gap also exists within the early childhood sector, by race, by type of setting providers work in, and by age of children whom providers serve (McLean et al., 2021). For example, Black early childhood educators are paid on average 78 cents less per hour than White early childhood educators. Center-based infant and toddler teachers make on average $8,375 less per year than preschool teachers and are more likely to be Black or Latina and immigrants (Center for the Study of Child Care Employment., 2020). These disparities affect teachers' and providers' ability to support their own families and may affect their mental health and wellness (Fináncz et al., 2020; Linnan et al., 2017). Childcare providers have elevated levels of stress and depression, compared to the general population (Elharake et al., 2022; Linnan et al. 2017; Whitaker et al., 2013). Mental health, in turn, is associated with the ways adults interact with children and is associated with harsh discipline (Gilliam & Shakar, 2006; Kwon et al., 2019; Silver & Zinsser, 2020).

Family leadership and engagement. High-quality programming is also characterized by holistic family leadership and engagement. In a high-quality education system, families' funds of knowledge, or the topics they are experts in, are embedded in the learning environment (Moll et al., 1990). Their holistic needs are supported, including their health and wellness, nutrition, and financial needs, and they are connected to community support services (e.g., McCarthy & Guerin, 2022). Families also have the opportunity to engage in leadership positions to ensure buy-in and accountability in the education system. To ensure families are engaged and have leadership positions, educators and administrators establish reciprocal relationships with families to build their trust, with information presented in families' home language(s) and preferred communication modalities (e.g., emails, texts, videos, flyers, etc.) (Trust for Learning, 2023). Families also are treated as partners and the first, and most important, educators that children will ever have.

Inclusion of children with disabilities. Although IDEA protects the rights of children ages 3–21 years old to a free and appropriate public education and infants and toddlers to early intervention, preschoolers and school-aged children with disabilities continue to receive segregated special education services, which continue to be an artifact of the institutionalization of children with disabilities in earlier decades (Peterson, 2016). National data have consistently shown that less than 50% of preschoolers with disabilities receive their services in general early childhood programs, with minimal change over time and recent regression over the course of the COVID-19 pandemic (US Department of Education, 2021). The number of school-aged children with disabilities receiving instruction with their peers without disabilities the majority of the day (80% or more of the day) has increased over time – from 59% to 66% between 2009 and 2020 (US Department of Education, 2021). Even with this growth, segregation of children with disabilities continues to persist (US Department of Education, 2022a).

A number of perceived and actual barriers contribute to districts' and schools' abilities to provide children with disabilities with services in inclusive settings. Commonly cited systemic barriers to inclusion include ableism (Shippen et al., 2005), perceived policy or financial barriers, lack of workforce preparation and professional development, uncoordinated services and systems, and lack of commitment (Leko & Brownell, 2009). Attitudes and beliefs about children with disabilities, undergirded by ableism, tend to be teachers' most cited barrier (Avramidis & Norwich, 2002; Fuchs, 2010). Additionally, there is an overall lack of coordination between special education systems and general early childhood systems, especially for young children with disabilities.

Inclusion is about physical placement and full meaningful participation and adequate support, high expectations, and appropriate accommodations (Council of Exceptional Children's Division for Early Childhood, 2014). The Division for Early Childhood has a set of recommended practices that provide guidance to practitioners about the most effective ways to promote the development of young children with disabilities. These practices include having a coordinated system that offers incentives for inclusion and child subsidies; having a written philosophy about inclusion; offering integrated professional development across disciplines; and having state and federal accountability systems to monitor inclusion. Another key set of practices that allows for the meaningful participation of children with disabilities is Universal Design for Learning (UDL; Center for Applied Special Technology, 2023). UDL is an instructional design framework that can be used to design curricula for students with and without disabilities across PK–12. When applying UDL, learning experiences are designed with the goal of reducing all barriers for all learners from the beginning of program development and instructional planning. The three main principles of UDL are to provide multiple means of engagement, representation, and action and expression. For example, if children are learning about metamorphosis, they might be presented with a video, picture, hands-on activities, museum visit, and so on to present the content using various modalities that fit each learner's needs. UDL has the potential to support meaningful inclusion of students in general educational settings (Rao et al., 2017).

Bilingual instruction for children who are dual language/English learners. Another important component of an equitable, high-quality education program is one that embraces and supports the bilingualism of DLLs/ELs. Bilingualism yields a host of cognitive, academic, social, and economic benefits over a person's lifetime (e.g., Gandara, 2015; Marian & Shook, 2012), and children with disabilities can also develop bilingually without causing confusion (Guiberson, 2013). Bilinguals can maintain stronger connections with their families and heritage and have stronger cross-cultural connections that expand their social networks (Boutakidis et al., 2011). They also enjoy cognitive advantages, with better inhibition and cognitive flexibility (Bialystok, 2011). Once older, bilinguals experience a five-and-half-year delay in the onset of Alzheimer's, as bilingualism serves as a buffer against cognitive decline (Craik et al., 2010).

For the benefits of bilingualism to be fully materialized, DLLs/ELs need to have additive bilingual instruction such as one-way or two-way dual language instruction, where the goal is to become bilingual, biliterate, bicultural, and conscious about societal inequities. Children and youth who are DLLs/ELs in preschool through high school who receive dual language instruction have higher language, reading, and math scores in both English and the other language than those who only receive English instruction (e.g., Barnett et al., 2007; Duran et al., 2010). For these children, the impressive benefits of dual language instruction are long-lasting. DLLs who attended a dual language program in preschool or kindergarten are less likely to be classified as an "English Learner" by middle school (Serafini et al., 2022; Steele et al., 2018). Steele and colleagues (2017) conducted a longitudinal study following the reading, math, and science performance of students enrolled in dual language programs from kindergarten to eighth grade in Portland public schools. Both students in two-way (50% of children speak English at home, 50% the partner language) and one-way immersion (100% of children speak the home language at home) programs had as high or higher reading scores than native English speakers in the same programs, without impacting their math or science skills negatively. By fifth and sixth grade, these students whose English was not their native language were more likely to no longer be classified as English learners, compared to those who did not receive dual language instruction. By eighth grade, students enrolled in these dual language programs had intermediate reading, speaking, listening, and writing fluency in their nonnative language. These findings accord with results that most children who completed a K–5

Spanish–English dual language immersion program continued taking Advanced Placement Spanish classes in high school, and nearly half earned the Seal of Biliteracy (Padilla, 2022). Moreover, these students had scores that were similar to or exceeded those of their DLL peers who only received English instruction on English language arts and math. These findings reveal the importance of providing English learners with high-quality dual language instruction. Despite the robust empirical research in favor of dual language instruction, most DLLs/ELs receive English-only instruction, or primarily English instruction with very limited use of their home language (e.g., Portes, 2002). These English-only approaches, which have historically been supported by law, are incongruent with best practices for bilingual children and youth. Widely accessible bilingual programming for PK–12 is an essential component of creating a sustainable education system prepared to meet the needs of a linguistically diverse nation such as the United States.

Mental health supports to foster social and emotional development and prevent harsh discipline. High-quality educational experiences require attention to children's mental health and intentional fostering of social and emotional development. Social development and emotional wellness serve as a foundation for learning and exploration. Children learn in the context of warm and secure relationships with adults and from their peers. Prioritizing the quality of adult–child and peer relationships through attention to social and emotional development is critical for children's development.

A lack of understanding of typical child development, including developmentally appropriate behavioral expectations, and lack of support for social and emotional development (for adults and children) can contribute to harsh discipline. Harsh discipline, including suspensions and expulsions, start as early as toddlerhood, happen frequently, and are disproportionately applied to Black children, boys, children with disabilities, and, in some cases, AI/AN and Latine children. Young preschool-age children are sometimes subjected to exclusionary discipline practices at rates higher than secondary age students.

Many variables contribute to the overuse of exclusionary discipline practices, with one in particular that stands out in the literature. Implicit bias manifests in many ways, including in increased scrutiny of particular groups of children, skewed perceptions of children's size, age, and intentions, and less favorable perceptions of the family. One study tracked teachers' eyes when they were asked to identify a challenging behavior when watching a video of children of different racial groups playing. No challenging behavior was present in the video, but given that instruction teachers were more likely to look at the Black boy in the video (Gilliam et al., 2016). Researchers have also found adultification bias in adults' perceptions of Black children. Adults rate Black girls as more mature and in less need of support (Epstein et al., 2017) and Black boys as being up to 4.5 years older than they are (Goff et al., 2014, Okonofua & Eberhardt, 2015). When given the same behavioral record with two different names – one a common name given to White babies in the state and one a common name given to Black babies in the state – teachers were more likely to recommend suspension for the fictitious child with a common Black name. This literature suggests greater scrutiny, adultification, and harsher discipline decisions associated with children's race or perceived race, not based on their actual behavior (Meek, et al., 2020).

Infant and early childhood mental health consultation (IECMCH) pairs early childhood mental health specialists with the adults who work with young children and families, including families, teachers, program directors, early interventionists and early childhood special educators, pediatricians, and others, to support children's social and emotional development and mental health. The approach is linked with reduced uses of exclusionary practices (Albritton et al., 2019; Conners-Burrow et al., 2012; Davis et al., 2020; Gilliam & Shahar, 2006; Upshur et al., 2009). The primary focus of IECMHC is to build the capacity of the adults – most often early educators – to develop comprehensive perspectives and strategies to enhance their interactions with young children (Kniegge-Tucker et al., 2020). IECMHC is a promising approach to support ECE teachers who work with culturally diverse children and assist with changing teachers' perceptions and behaviors (Davis et al., 2020b). In general, teachers who have access to IECMHC tend to report decreases in children's challenging behavior, improved classroom quality, and enhanced teacher–child interactions (i.e., increases in closeness and decreases in conflict) (Albritton et al., 2019).

Positive behavior intervention and supports (PBIS) increases social emotional development and decreases challenging behavior and exclusionary discipline. Recent work has begun to infuse equity explicitly into the PBIS model through new resources produced from the federally funded National Center on PBIS. PBIS is associated with narrowing racial disparities in addition to lowering overall rates of exclusionary discipline (McIntosh et al., 2021a, 2021b). The pyramid model is an early childhood PBIS model that is widely implemented in the United States. It focuses on promoting social emotional development, improving classroom management, and supporting the inclusion of young children with disabilities in inclusive settings (Hemmeter et al., 2021; 2022).

3.5 Conclusion

The systematic, historical exclusion and segregation of Black, Latine, Indigenous children, immigrant children, children with disabilities, and others in our education system has contributed to the creation and maintenance of the racial and ability disparities in educational outcomes that we see today. These children and their families deserve an education that centers their needs, strengths, identities, and values. Offering these children with high quality education is multifaceted, ranging from child-centered pedagogies that are asset-focused, comprehensive early learning standards that are not based on White norms, a well-compensated and culturally and linguistically diverse workforce, data-driven instruction, strong family leadership and engagement, and positive guidance and behavior supports.

4 Equity in Children's Health and Well-Being

The concept of health equity entails ensuring that every child, especially those who have been marginalized in the past and presently, has the necessary resources and conditions to develop and thrive fully. This includes access to high-quality health care, mental health support and nutritious food in both health care systems and public health, and safe environments. This section examines the historical perspective of health system inequalities and how these affect children and families. It delves into the role of social determinants of health and adverse childhood experiences (ACES), highlighting how children's health is impacted by their living, playing, and learning environments, as well as their experiences in those spaces. Additionally, it covers contemporary health issues, such as the impact of the COVID-19 pandemic, as well as disproportionalities in maternal and child health outcomes.

4.1 Health Equity for Children

Health equity, in the context of child equity, means all children, particularly those historically and contemporaneously marginalized, have the necessary support and conditions to live healthy lives that enable them to reach their full potential. Achieving health equity requires children and families to have access to high-quality health care, nutritious food, and safe environments free from toxins. Fair distribution of resources is also important, including equal opportunities for education and economic well-being, as these are social determinants of health. Camara Jones (2014) asserts health equity will be achieved when each individual is valued and health disparities have been eliminated. Uneven opportunity and differences in access to health care, nutritious food, and healthy and safe environments contribute to poor health outcomes for children from historically marginalized communities and their families and create or perpetuate preventable health disparities between these children and their more advantaged peers. Indeed, Flores and colleagues (2010) at the American Academy of Pediatrics concluded that "racial/ethnic disparities in child health and health care are extensive, pervasive, and persistent, and occur across the spectrum of health and health care" (Flores, 2010).

We cannot consider the broader history of health systems in the United States and its relation to children's health equity without considering the role of social determinants. Social determinants of health are conditions in the environment where children are born, live, play, learn, and age. Although an exhaustive review is beyond the scope of this Element, we highlight major examples in nutrition, health care, and environmental health to better understand children's health disparities and health equity. We have placed particular emphasis on maternal and child health and mental health, considering the well-documented stark disparities and profound effects they have on children's developmental trajectories. We take an historical approach to understanding health outcomes in children's equity today, in the context of US health systems.

4.2 Social Determinants of Health

Children's health is impacted by where they live, play, and learn and their experiences in those spaces. The Center for Disease Control and Protection refers to these factors as the social determinants of health (SDOH). Upwards of 80% of children's health is impacted by factors outside of the health care system (Manatt & Phillips, 2019). The CDC groups SDOH into five domains: economic stability, education access and quality, health care access and quality, neighborhood and built environment, and social and community context. Inequities across domains of SDOH have unduly burdened communities of color with high rates of chronic diseases, high blood pressure, and asthma – factors that most recently have put these communities at an increased risk for developing severe COVID-19 complications.

The CDC and research confirm that experiencing racism is a social determinant of health in itself and impacts every other SDOH domain, like access to affordable and safe housing (Yearby, 2021). It is well documented through hundreds of empirical studies that racial discrimination, ranging from day-to-day indignities like receiving poor service at a restaurant to mistreatment by medical professionals to fear of police brutality are associated with increased rates of chronic diseases, such as heart disease (Ansell & McDonald 2015; Trent et al., 2019). The impacts of racism are linked to poor birth outcomes and mental health problems in infants, children, and adolescents (Trent et al., 2019). Furthermore, structural sexism (i.e., mistreatment by health care professionals, "everyday" sexual harassment, gendered power and resource inequities) contribute to mothers' use of health care services, which impacts health outcomes

(Homan, 2019; McDonald, 2012; Pavalko et al., 2003). For example, data indicate that expectant parents of color who report experiencing discrimination are more likely to give birth to low birthweight babies (Earnshaw et al., 2013; Guirgescu et al., 2011).

Social determinants of health specifically impact children with disabilities and their families. To have full participation in society, children with disabilities need coordinated care with access to health insurance and families with the resources to support them (King et al., 2023). Social determinants that promote families' capacity to support their children with disabilities include having financial security, a positive home environment, and opportunities for recreation. Children also need access to multidisciplinary coordinated care including medical treatments (when relevant), therapies, and inclusive learning and social opportunities (King et al., 2003). Unfortunately, this coordinated care is mediated by families' income, access to health insurance, and their marital status (Pankewicz et al., 2020), with access to coordinated care even more challenging for children with disabilities and their families (Newacheck et al., 2002). Newacheck and colleagues (2002) found that Black and Latine children with disabilities were more likely to be without health coverage, and their parents reported the inability to receive medical care for them. These findings underscore the importance of ensuring children with disabilities and their families have the environmental, social, health, and financial support they need to thrive. Other major social determinants of health, including family economic well-being and educational and learning opportunities, are covered in more depth in sections 2 and 3.

4.3 Adverse Childhood Experiences

Adverse childhood experiences (ACEs) are negative traumatic experiences in childhood that impact children's long-term health, well-being, and academic outcomes (Felitti et al., 1998). ACEs include physical/emotional/sexual abuse, household mental illness, household substance use, household domestic violence, an incarcerated household member, and parental separation/divorce. Individuals who experience four or more ACEs, even at conception, are more likely to experience adult diseases and disorders like hypertension, depression, substance abuse, and diabetes, as well as the attainment of lower wages and educational opportunities (Felitti et al., 1998; Merrick et al., 2019). Racial, ethnic, and income differences exist in the frequency of ACEs individuals experience. For example, Black children and adults experience the most ACEs compared to Latine, White, and Asian families, and families from low to middle incomes are more likely to have two or more ACEs than those in higher incomes (Giano et al., 2020). These findings underscore the importance of identifying the roles of racism and poverty on ACEs and their impact on the health outcomes of children. Preliminary evidence suggests that the negative effects of ACEs can be transmitted from one generation to the next (Buss et al., 2017; Monk et al., 2016). Toxic stress experienced by women during pregnancy can negatively affect fetal development, which can contribute to a host of negative outcomes, sometimes much later in life (Child Trends, 2018). Some scholars have critiqued the ACEs framework for its exclusion of discrimination and racism and their impact on children's health development (e.g., Cronholm et al., 2015; Wade et al., 2014). Several others have extended the ACEs framework to include racism-related indicators, pointing to the well-established connection between racism and discrimination with toxic stress, poor health, and a host of mental health outcomes (i.e., depression, anxiety, hypervigilance; Bernard et al., 2021). Bernard and colleagues (2021) proposed including racial trauma as an ACE, because racism has a multifaceted, compounding impact on the health of Black children.

ACEs have serious, long-lasting, and multigenerational impacts on children. However, ACEs can be prevented and addressed through structured and systemic interventions to support families' economic stability, access to high-quality care and education, access to health care, including mental health supports, and the availability of other social programs.

4.4 Environmental Health

Environmental health is the relation between people's health and their environment, such as their neighborhood's air quality, clean water, and safe housing. These environmental factors constitute a major social determinant of health and have, both historically and contemporaneously, been impacted by policies and practices. Indeed, environmental racism, or policy and resource decisions made to advantage White communities while disadvantaging communities of color, is a major driver of health inequities (Henderson & Wells, 2021).

One major health inequity that impacts communities of color is exposure to environmental toxins. These environmental toxins include exposure to pollution – which goes beyond but cannot be separated from efforts to build large highways and traffic areas through and adjacent to Black communities, less access to clean water – which is associated with the under-investments in community infrastructure, and closer proximity to toxic waste (Hajat et al., 2021; Taylor, 2014). A 2018 report by the Environmental Protection Agency revealed, "results at national, state, and county scales all indicate that non-White people tend to be burdened by air pollution disproportionately to White people" (Tessum et al., 2018, p. 484).

People of color are disproportionately exposed to breathing polluted air, which can result in an increased risk of developing lung and heart disease – a disease that is more acute for children and youth (WHO, 2005). For example, Black children are 2.2 times more likely to suffer from asthma than their White peers (Office of Minority Health, 2018). In fact, Black, Latine, and AI/AN people have the highest rates of hospitalization and death associated with asthma. Other health issues associated with the environment – including air and water quality – are cancer and lead poisoning (Gee & Payne-Sturgers, 2004).

Lead exposure, in particular, can have serious and chronic effects on development and learning (CDC, 2022). According to the Center for Disease Control and Prevention, fewer than 34% of children were tested for lead exposure between January and May 2020, during the COVID-19 pandemic (Courtney et al., 2021). National data indicate that the presence of lead in blood screenings is above the recommended safe threshold for 2.5% of children tested; however, these rates vary by state, with some states having over 10% of children testing positive for lead exposure. Black children and those living in low-income households are at higher risk of lead exposure compared to their White peers (Miranda et al., 2009; Perry et al., 2021). Similar patterns are observed among expecting parents, with studies finding higher levels of lead among Black and Latine expecting parents compared to White expecting parents (Miranda et al., 2009; Perry et al., 2021). Exposure to lead for Black and Latine expecting parents is especially alarming as lead is very harmful to developing fetuses and young children, affecting their physical and cognitive development (CDC, 2022).

One factor underlying the disproportionate exposure to environmental toxins (such as lead and polluted air) is the residential segregation of Black Americans and other people of color historically and today. For example, communities with majority people of color, even when controlling for economic factors and other demographic variables, tend to have higher infant mortality rates, asthma rates, tuberculosis, adverse birth outcomes, and decreased life expectancy (Acevedo-Garcia, 2003; Gee et al., 2004; Swope, 2022). These communities also face increased exposure to tobacco and alcohol advertising (US Department of Health and Human Services, 1998).

The residential segregation of Black, Latine, AI/AN, and other people of color is historically rooted and has pervasive, negative outcomes on children's health. For example, redlining and other mechanisms of segregation and exclusion have contributed to families of color living in concentrated urban areas that have reduced access to resources and poorer environmental conditions associated with reduced health outcomes (Christie-Mizell, 2022). Historical and contemporary underinvestment in these communities, inadequate environmental regulation and/or enforcement, close proximity to pollution sources, and insufficient response to communities' concerns about environmental toxins have over generations contributed to less healthy living conditions. Together, these policies and practices put families at greater risk of adverse health outcomes, such as respiratory illnesses, asthma, high blood pressure, and heart disease (Benfer & Lindsay 2020; Gee et al., 2004; Lopez, 2002; Scholar Institute of Medicine, 1999).

Exposure to environmental toxins – whether through air, water, or physical space – can be particularly harmful to young children who are early in their development and in a highly sensitive period of neural development. Moreover, greater health challenges in families and in primary caregivers affect children in many ways, including by influencing the amount of time and activity level parents can engage in with them, and burden families with greater medical costs and the potential for lower employment prospects, decreasing economic well-being. These environmental conditions are associated with disparities in life expectancy and early adult mortality, which influence whether children have a living parent or parents to rear them at all.

Policymakers are establishing policies and programs to address historical and contemporary environmental inequities that lead to disparities in health outcomes. Several US states have implemented more robust processes for determining where certain facilities can be erected to mitigate the impacts on affected communities, most of which are communities of color. For instance, in 2020, New Jersey required the Department of Environmental Protection to consider the environmental and public health impacts of particular facilities, including gas-fired power plants, wastewater treatment plants, and landfills, when reviewing facilities permit applications. As a result of this law, New Jersey is now the first state to require state agencies to deny permits to new industrial, commercial, and governmental facilities if an analysis determines those facilities will have a disproportionately negative impact on the surrounding community (National Conference of State Legislatures [NCSL], 2022). A number of states, including Massachusetts and Rhode Island, have considered policies to regulate the location of certain facilities and improve the processes for determining how land can be used (Perls, 2020). In 2021, President Biden signed the Infrastructure Investment and Jobs Act, which included over $50 billion to invest in clean water in homes, schools, childcare programs, and businesses. In 2023, the US Environmental Protection Agency and Health and Human Services published guidance to states and communities to prevent and mitigate toxic exposure to lead in early care and education programs, including through contaminated drinking water (Office of Early Childhood Development, 2023).

4.5 Food and Nutrition

Access to healthy and nutritious foods is also associated with a host of positive outcomes for families and children, namely improved infant and maternal health and reductions in food insecurity. In 2020, according to the Economic Research Service (ERS) of the United States Department of Agriculture (USDA), thirty-four million people, including nine million children, lived in food insecure households (USDA, 2022). Black and Latine children are more than twice as likely to be food insecure than their White peers (USDA, 2021).

Structural inequality like housing and employment discrimination have contributed to children of color living in poverty and facing food insecurity (Benfer & Lindsay 2020; Ke & Ford-Jones, 2015). Children living in food-insecure homes are more likely to suffer harmful impacts to their physical growth and social development, including delays in physical and cognitive development, poor academic outcomes, and mental health challenges (Gallegos et al., 2021).

Counties in the United States with above-average Black populations tend to have fewer fresh food options, but more convenience stores (USDA Food Atlas, 2020). Latine communities also have a higher prevalence of small grocery and convenience stores (Ohri-Vachaspati et al., 2019). In contrast, counties with higher populations of White people have more access to choices, including farmers' markets, restaurants, grocery stores, and fewer convenience stores. There is a significant link between proximity to supermarkets and grocery stores and the consumption of fruits and vegetables (Fiechtner et al., 2016; Gase et al., 2014). These inequities are consequential to children and families' abilities to access healthy food.

Food assistance programs, including the Supplemental Nutrition Assistance Program (SNAP) and the Women, Infant, and Child (WIC) program, were launched in 1974 to address barriers to access healthy food. SNAP provides monthly benefits for individuals and families that can be used to purchase food, and WIC provides fresh produce, formula, and breastfeeding support to expectant mothers, breastfeeding mothers, and mothers of young children up to age five. WIC is especially important for marginalized populations and communities who have reduced access to full-service grocery stores that sell fresh produce and nutritious food (Sansom & Hannibal, 2021). The US Department of Agriculture, which oversees SNAP and WIC, reports that SNAP enrollment reduced food insecurity (Mabli et al., 2013). Researchers have also found a lower likelihood of low birthweight babies among SNAP recipients compared to their peers of similar incomes who did not receive nutrition support, with greater impacts on Black mothers (Almond et al., 2011). Data indicate that the effects of SNAP go beyond nutrition, with young children in households that receive SNAP achieving better math and reading scores and missing fewer school days, compared to children who were in poverty prior to their receipt of SNAP (Hong & Henley, 2020).

4.6 Health Insurance and Health Care

Access to affordable health insurance and quality health care is foundational to healthy development and child equity. Still, universal health insurance and health care are not universally accessible in the United States. Lack of insurance is highest among Latine children, children from families with low-incomes, and children living in states that did not pass legislation to expand Medicaid (Alker, 2020). Uninsured children have more health challenges such as unmet medical and dental needs, more hospitalizations, and higher in-hospital mortality rates (Paradise, 2014).

Three major efforts have been made to increase access to health insurance: Medicaid, the Children's Health Insurance Program (CHIP), and the Affordable Care Act (ACA). Medicaid was signed into law in 1965 and is administered differently across states, creating variations in coverage. Medicaid programs are designed to provide health coverage for children and families from low-income backgrounds. Expansions of the program during the 1980s and 1990s made Medicaid the largest single insurance provider for families and children from low-income backgrounds in the United States (Morrisey, 2013). Additionally, Medicaid coverage has had positive impacts on expecting parents. Mothers with access to Medicaid had reduced maternal mortality rates, fewer low birthweight babies, and fewer childhood deaths (Kreider et al., 2016). In 2020, Medicaid covered nearly half of all births in the United States, including 65% of Black and AI/AN births, 59% of Latine births, and just 30% of White births. Medicaid also provides health insurance coverage for 48% of children with special health care needs (Artiga et al., 2022b).

Prior to the passage of CHIP in 1997, the child uninsured rate was 14% (Cornachione et al., 2016). Today, seven million children (42%) are covered by CHIP. Between 1997 and 2014, Medicaid and CHIP decreased the uninsured rate from 14% to a historic low of 6%. The child uninsured rate in 2022 is 5% (Mykyta et al., 2022). Still, millions of children remain uninsured, and these figures differ by group. AI/AN children (13%) are over three times as likely as their White counterparts to be uninsured, and Latine children are over twice as likely as White children to be uninsured (8.6% vs. 4.0%; Artiga et al., 2022). Health insurance coverage, private or public, is particularly difficult for immigrant children who are undocumented. In 2022, reports estimated that over 2.3 million children were disallowed from receiving public health insurance despite income eligibility because of their categorization as undocumented immigrants. Currently, eleven states plus Washington, DC, allow children without documentation to be eligible for Medicaid or CHIP (Garfield, 2020; Lacarte, 2022). Still, about one-half of undocumented children, otherwise eligible for Medicaid, are uninsured, compared with 6% of US-born children (Garfield, 2020). People, regardless of immigration status, can now access prenatal care in eighteen states (Garfield, 2020; Lacarte, 2022).

In 2022, children accounted for 43% of the eighty-eight million individuals enrolled in Medicaid and CHIP (Centers for Medicare and Medicaid Services, 2022). Across states, children participating in CHIP live in families whose incomes range from 170% to 400% of the federal poverty line. More than half (57%) of all Black children use CHIP or Medicaid for health care coverage, compared to just 33% of White children (Brooks & Gardner, 2020). Relative to their population size, Black, Latine, and AI/AN children comprised 20%, 25%, and 1.5% of children covered by Medicaid or CHIP in 2016, respectively (Georgetown University Health Policy Institute, 2018).

In 2010, President Obama signed the ACA into law, which reformed the US health care system by expanding and enhancing health insurance coverage and increasing the quality of care. The ACA had significant impacts on the quality of health care by including provisions to cover women's and children's preventive services at no cost-sharing, eliminating exclusions for preexisting conditions, and prohibiting lifetime dollar limits, which improved access for children with special health care needs (Gunja et al., 2017). Particularly important to child well-being and children's equity, the ACA decreased the uninsured rate among women ages 19–34 by more than 10 percentage points, from 25% in 2010 to 14% in 2016 (Gunja et al., 2017).

Part of the signature law included Medicaid expansion. As of 2023, most states and DC have expanded Medicaid coverage through the ACA (Rudowitz et al., 2019). Seven of the ten states that have not expanded coverage are southern states – Texas, Mississippi, Tennessee, Alabama, Georgia, South Carolina, and Florida. Of note, the South has the highest share of the country's Black population, with 56% of this population living there, compared to 17% in the northeast and Midwest and 10% in the west (Tamir, 2021). There are clear insurance access trends between expansion and non-expansion states. For example, the uninsured rate for Latine parents is 20.9% in expansion states compared to 38.2% in non-expansion states. Latine children in non-expansion states are 2.5 times more likely to be uninsured.

Despite the benefits of having health insurance, children with disabilities and chronic health conditions experience barriers in quality and access to health care services. These families report lower rates of access to care in their community and inadequate insurance (Cheak-Zamora et al., 2017). Data from the National Survey of Children with Special Health Care Needs revealed that Black and Latine families of children with autism and other developmental disorders experience a lower quality of care compared to their White peers (Liptak et al., 2008). For example, Black children with autism are less likely to have a personal doctor than White children, and Black and Latine parents report that their children's doctors do not listen to them fully. These findings accord with those of Ereniz-Wiemer and colleagues (2014), who found that children with disabilities whose parents had limited English fluency were more likely to experience poorer health outcomes. These findings illustrate the intersectionality of race and ethnicity, disability, and access to adequate health care.

There have been significant efforts to increase access to health care, but children and families' experiences and outcomes are not consistent across race and ethnicity. A robust body of research reveals several barriers that impact equitable access to health care, including access to reliable transportation, challenges accessing trusted pediatric care, limited culturally and linguistically responsive physicians, and affordability and accessibility of health insurance (Alker, 2020; Syed et al., 2013). Moreover, barriers to affordable health coverage have resulted in racialized disparities in health outcomes such as life expectancy, chronic diseases, and maternal and infant mortality rates (Perrin et al., 2020).

Access to affordable, stable, and quality health care increases the opportunity for families to provide a pathway to optimal health for their children and is associated with improved health outcomes. Data from the American Community Survey of 2021 and the 2020–2021 National Survey of Children's Health found that about 9% of Latine children and 7% of Black children did not have access to routine health care when they were sick, compared to 4% of White children. Latine (12%) and Asian (11%) families were more likely to report going without a health care visit in the past year than White (8%) and Black families (7%). When children do not have access to timely health care, they are vulnerable to increased medical complications and chronic diseases (Institute of Medicine, 2009). They are also more likely to use the emergency room for care, which increases the cost-of-service delivery (Taylor & Salyakina, 2019). The lack of accessible health insurance and affordable health care in the United States affects the lives of millions of children and their families and further entrenches health disparities. Indeed, equity for children requires accessible, affordable, consistent, and quality care for children and their families to reach their full potential.

4.7 Maternal and Child Health

Children's equity begins with access to quality prenatal, perinatal, and postpartum care for expecting parents. This includes accessible and affordable care, regular visits with a health care provider (i.e., OBGYN, midwife, doula), partnering in decision-making, and quality unbiased health care from the prenatal through the perinatal period. Despite the advances in medical technology and several targeted public health interventions, the United States has one of the worst maternal death rates of any wealthy nation in the world. In 2021, 1,205 women and nearly 20,000 babies died due to pregnancy-related causes (Hoyert, 2023; Xu et al., 2014). Maternal mortality rates were notably higher in 2020 and 2021, compared to previous years, with about a quarter of maternal deaths being attributed to COVID-19 in 2021. Still, rates have been increasing steadily since 2018 (Centers for Disease Control and Prevention, 2022; Government Accountability Office, 2022). The CDC notes that 80% of maternal deaths are preventable (Trost et al., 2019).

The CDC reports infant and maternal mortality rates vary significantly by race, with AI/AN women being two to three times more likely to die of pregnancy-related causes than White women, and Black women being four times more likely (Peterson, 2016). These racial disparities are long-standing. In 1920, there was a 43% difference between Black infant mortality and White infant mortality. Nearly a century later, infant mortality rates for Black infants (10.62%) remain two times higher than those for White (4.49%), Asian (3.38%), and Latine (5.03%) infants (Davis et al., 1987; Ely & Driscoll, 2021). Likewise, AI/AN and Puerto Rican expecting parents also experience higher rates of infant mortality than their White counterparts (Horan et al., 2021).

One factor that impacts racial disparities in infant mortality is the lack of or limited access to prenatal care. About 77% of all expecting parents received prenatal care in 2016 (Perrin et al. 2020). Between 2018 and 2020, about 68%, 72%, and 64% of Black, Latine, and AI/AN pregnant women, respectively, received early prenatal care, compared to 82% and 81% of White and Asian American Pacific Islander women, respectively (March of Dimes, 2023). These disparities are driven by a complex set of challenges that disproportionately impact families of color, including lack of universal insurance coverage, the shortage of providers serving historically marginalized communities, and other barriers that impact individuals' ability to access timely care, such as inadequate transportation, inflexible work schedules, and lack of paid sick leave benefits.

Bias is another contributing factor to disparities in maternal and infant mortality. Bias occurs at both interpersonal and institutional levels. Physicians have implicit biases, as well as explicit biases, each of which have serious negative consequences for the health and well-being of their patients (Saluja & Bryant, 2021). These explicit and implicit biases are shaped by structural forms of discrimination including racism, sexism, ableism, and so on (Hall et al., 2015). The American College of Obstetricians and Gynecologists (2022) acknowledges that bias in the health care system contributes to the inequitable health outcomes of Black and AI/AN families prenatally, during birth, and postnatally. These biases have serious negative consequences, including a failure to respond to Black patients' pain (Hoffman et al., 2016), as well as OBGYNs' decisions about treatment options, counseling about C-section after vaginal delivery, and management of gestational chronic conditions (Saluja & Bryant, 2021). One study found that when Black infants are cared for by a Black doctor, the mortality rate, compared to White babies, is cut in half (Greenwood, Hardeman et al., 2020). Physicians are not the only ones with bias. A variety of health care employees also have and act on biases. For example, lactation support staff is more likely to recommend Black parents to use formula than White parents, despite recommendation by the American Academy of Pediatrics to breastfeed all infants for at least six months (McKinney et al., 2016).

Many decisions made during the labor and delivery process are subjective, and therefore can be impacted by bias (Fitzgerald & Hurst, 2017). One of those decisions is whether a delivery should occur vaginally or through a cesarean delivery (C-section). Cesarean deliveries are associated with higher maternal mortality rates and maternal morbidity (Caughey et al., 2014). C-sections are associated with three of the six leading causes of pregnancy-related deaths: hemorrhage, complications of anesthesia, and infection (Roth & Henley, 2012). Yet, in 2011 one in three women delivered by C-section (Hamilton, 2013). In 2017, the C-section rate for Black women was 36% compared to 30.9% for White women. This overrepresentation of C-section deliveries highlights flaws in the health care system that place lives at risk during labor in ways that are often unnecessary.

Although interpersonal racism is a driver of racial disparities in maternal and infant mortality rates, systemic inequities including significant underinvestment in family support and health care programs also contribute to the alarming trends in maternal and infant health (Bruner & Johnson, 2018). Federal under-investment results in disparities in proximity to quality, timely care for millions of families. According to the March of Dimes (2018), over 12% of births occur in maternity care deserts, which are locations with limited access to maternity care and is particularly acute for residents in rural counties. More than one-half of rural counties lack access to obstetric care (Hung et al., 2017). Rural counties with families who have low incomes and more Black residents are even less likely to have hospitals with obstetric services (Hung et al., 2017).

Finally, factors outside of the immediate health care system also contribute to disparities in maternal and child health outcomes. Black and Latine families are less likely to have access to nutritious food and are more likely to be exposed to environmental toxins, like air pollution. Black, AI/AN, and Latine families are also more likely to experience poverty, making reliable transportation, safe and stable housing, and adequate nutrition more difficult. Experiencing racism also has health consequences, particularly on maternal health. The American Psychological Association (APA, 2012) released the *Ethnicity and Health in America Series*, detailing discrimination and racism's psychological impact on stress, arguing that racism is a form of chronic stress. Chronic stress results in increased cortisol levels, which cause high blood pressure. Chronic stress is also associated with depression, which can be associated with higher risks for preeclampsia, gestational diabetes, and low birth weight (Somerville et al., 2021). This chronic stress is particularly alarming for Black women, who, research indicates, experience a process known as weathering (Geronimus, 1992). Weathering suggests that chronic financial strain (Simons et al., 2016) and racial discrimination (Geronimus, 1992) lead to premature aging for Black women, leaving even young Black expecting parents at higher risk for chronic pregnancy-related conditions (Geronimus et al., 2006). Black women face a higher risk of various medical conditions due to the long-term psychological impact of racism. These conditions can threaten the lives of both the mother and her infant, including preeclampsia, eclampsia, embolism, and mental health disorders. In one study, weathering was also linked to low birth weight in Black infants (Geronimus, 1992). It is important for future public health initiatives to take into account the role of discrimination on the inequities in maternal and child health.

Across the country, major initiatives are in place to address the infant and maternal mortality crisis, including mandating implicit bias training for resident physicians, as well as practicing physicians, including health equity indicators as measures of ranking for hospitals. For example, California passed two bills mandating health care providers to attend implicit bias training: Assembly Bill 241 and Senate Bill 464. Assembly Bill 241, passed in 2022, requires all continuing education courses for physicians and surgeons to include content on implicit bias in medical treatment. Senate Bill 464, the California Dignity in Pregnancy and Childbirth Act, passed in 2020 and mandates implicit bias education for any health care professional providing perinatal services. Maryland, Michigan, and Washington have also passed similar bills to disrupt the negative impact of implicit bias in the health care system.

Expanding access to birth options to include the care of midwives and doulas has been a powerful intervention in decreasing maternal and infant mortality in the United States. Doula support during pregnancy, birth, and the postpartum period reduces rates of cesarean deliveries, prematurity and illness in newborns, and the likelihood of postpartum depression (Wint et al., 2019). Doula care also improves overall satisfaction with the experience of childbirth care and increases breastfeeding initiation and duration. Providing teams of midwives and doulas that apply relationship-focused, culturally responsive care is associated with decreases in preterm birth weights (Joseph, 2020).

Despite the benefits of having alternative birthing care, such as doulas, there is inequitable access to who has access to them (Knocke et al., 2022; Safon et al., 2021). To address this inequity, many states are expanding Medicaid benefits to cover doula services. As of June 2022, six states (Oregon, Minnesota, New Jersey, Florida, Maryland, and Virginia) currently reimburse doula services in Medicaid (Clark & Burak, 2022). In addition, six states (California, Washington, DC, Illinois, Indiana, Nevada, and Rhode Island) plan to cover doulas under Medicaid by 2023 (Clark & Burak, 2022). Ensuring equitable access to expanded culturally responsive birth options is necessary to address racial and class health disparities.

4.8 Mental Health and Well-Being of Children and Families

Mental health refers to emotional, psychological, and social well-being. Each positive and negative experience beginning in utero throughout childhood and adolescence impacts lifelong wellness. Historical, social, and political traumas or significant events, such as the enslavement of African peoples, the violent colonization of AI/AN peoples, internment camps for Japanese people, the Holocaust, the institutionalization of people with disabilities, and punitive immigration policies have resulted in psychological and emotional trauma for some members of the affected communities. These traumas need to be considered as we reflect on the current realities facing children and families and their disproportionate impact on mental health.

Mental illnesses are among the most common health conditions in the United States, with more than 50% of individuals diagnosed with a mental illness at some point in their lifetime (Kessler et al., 2007). Living in low-income households or low-income communities has been linked to increased risk for mental health problems in both children and adults that can persist across the life span (Hodgkinson et al., 2017). Despite their high need for mental health support, these children and families are least likely to be connected with timely, high-quality mental health care. It is estimated that among children experiencing poverty who are in need of mental health care, fewer than 15% receive services, and even fewer complete treatment (Bitzco et al., 2022). Although there is no significant difference in the prevalence of mental health problems among children residing in poverty by race or geographic residence, there are significant disparities in mental health service utilization across racial and ethnic groups and urbanicity (Howell & McFeeters, 2008). Studies have generally found lower mental health service utilization among Black and Latine children, compared with White children (Kataoka et al., 2002; Zahner, & Daskalakis, 1997).

Trends indicate rising symptoms of anxiety and depression among children in the US, with 10–16% of children experiencing a mental illness. Prior to the pandemic, national data showed that one in five children between six and seventeen years of age experiences a mental health disorder in a given year. However, the pandemic exacerbated the mental health crisis. Between March and June of 2020, more than 25% of parents reported that their child experienced declines in mental health and 14% reported increases in behavior problems (Department of Education, 2021). Pregnant mothers also faced an increase in Post-traumatic stress disorder (PTSD), depression, and anxiety, with some data indicating that during the COVID-19 pandemic, pregnant mothers' instances of depression doubled (Barbosa-Leiker et al., 2021).

Barriers to mental health treatment cited in the literature include clinic hours, which are more often during the day and are less likely to accommodate workers with unpredictable work schedules or shift workers with less flexible schedules (Levy & O'Hara, 2010), long wait times for appointments (Goodman et al., 2013), lack of mental health professionals of color and culturally responsive mental health care (Wyse et al., 2020), lack of prior experiences with mental health treatment (Ward et al., 2013), previous experiences with racism and discrimination in mental health treatment (Rhodes, 2023), prior experiences with mental health treatment (Ward et al., 2013), lack of insurance coverage, and providers not accepting patients who use Medicaid. Data from the 2019 Medicare and CHIP Payment and Access Commission (MACPAC) reported that 62% of psychiatrists accepted new patients with private insurance and Medicare, whereas only 36% accepted new patients with Medicaid. Disparities exist even within Medicaid services, with children of color who are covered by Medicaid or CHIP being significantly less likely to access any form of behavioral health services than their White counterparts covered by Medicaid (Bowers, 2021). Data further indicate that a significantly lower percentage of first-generation Latine youth (18%) accesses behavioral health services compared to Latine youth of

US-born parents (35%). Another barrier to treatment, particularly for communities of color, may be the lack of diversity in the mental health workforce. According to the American Psychiatric Association, Black mental health professionals represent only about 2% of practicing psychiatrists and 4% of psychologists providing care.

There are also disparities when examining treatment. Latine youth are among the most likely to experience depression, higher than any other group except AI/AN youth, with over one-third having a clinical need for mental health treatment. Stress for this group of children includes family and community level stressors as well as fears and worries about immigration enforcement, which is particularly acute in mixed status or undocumented families (Robert Wood Johnson Foundation, 2017). Barriers to treatment include a lack of culturally responsive and bilingual service providers, lack of comprehensive insurance coverage, and fears of interacting with public systems because of immigration enforcement (Alegria et al., 2002).

Less than 40% of children with mental health needs receive mental health services, with children of color more likely to have unmet mental health care needs compared to White children (American Psychological Association, 2012). Women of color report experiencing postpartum mental illness at higher rates than White women and are less likely to receive treatment (Keefe et al., 2018). Although women of all racial and ethnic backgrounds experience mental health disorders during and after pregnancy, Black women may be at higher risk for these illnesses because of the experiences with racism and discrimination (Rhodes, 2023). According to the Maternal Mental Health Leadership Alliance, Black women are twice as likely as White women to experience maternal mental health conditions, but they are half as likely to receive treatment (Dumessa & Kaplan, 2022).

Resources to address child mental health needs vary across schools, programs, and districts often focus on crisis management and reactive responses to individual child issues rather than a comprehensive system of support (Department of Education, 2021). Despite these challenges, many school staff have limited mental health knowledge and schools rely on community-based mental health services to provide and/or supplement their school mental health supports (Department of Education, 2021). Moreover, there is a shortage of mental health support staff, like counselors and psychologists, in schools. Over 90% of students attend schools with student-to-counselor ratios exceeding levels recommended by the American School Counselor Association, with about one-quarter of schools reporting having no counselor at all, affecting upwards of eight million children (Mann et al., 2019).

4.9 Impact of the COVID-19 Pandemic on Health and Wellness

The pandemic had a profound impact on children and families' health and well-being (Graham, 2021), exacerbating long entrenched racial health disparities. Drivers for these disparities were complex and are not yet fully understood, but include unequal access to medical care and vaccinations, overrepresentation in essential non-remote work, and living in smaller physical spaces without the ability to isolate. For example, in the United States, people who are Latine are the largest population from an historically and contemporaneously marginalized community, comprising 18% of the population. However, they represented 28% of COVID cases reported to the CDC. Latine families also faced challenges related to immigration status, as some families could not apply for public assistance, such as Temporary Assistance for Needy Families (TANF), and others had reduced access to medical care. Additional challenges included having language barriers that made it difficult to communicate their needs in medical settings due to limited personnel who spoke their language. As a result, they were more likely to experience longer medical stays and more visits to emergency departments, and have poorer clinical outcomes (Obinna, 2021).

An estimated 216,617 children lost a caregiver who died of COVID-19 in the United States as of May 2022. This was about 1 out of every 336 US Americans under eighteen years old (American Academy of Pediatrics, 2021; Treglia et al., 2022). The majority of these children (97,738) lost a parent, while nearly 85,000 children experienced the death of a grandparent caregiver (Treglia et al., 2022). Twenty percent of children experiencing caregiver loss were from birth through four years old; 50% were children ages five through thirteen years old, and the remaining 29% were children fourteen through seventeen years old (Treglia et al., 2022). Families of color were hit especially hard. They experienced up to 4.5 times the risk of losing a caregiver to COVID, compared to other children (American Academy of Pediatrics, 2021). Disparities based on race/ethnicity were strongest for the youngest children. For example, one study found that AI/AN children under five years old had caregiver loss rates 4.6 times that of their White peers (Treglia et al., 2022). Similar age-based trends were apparent for Latine and Black children. The loss of a caregiver can bring immense trauma to a child of any age but may be particularly traumatic and disruptive to the development and well-being of a young child who is fully and solely dependent on their primary caregiver.

4.10 Conclusion

Family and children's access to bias-conscious, high-quality health care is pivotal for their overall well-being. Unfortunately, like the economic and education systems, families and children of color, as well as children with disabilities, have less access to comprehensive, high-quality medical care and more negative experiences within the health system. To ensure these children and families have access to optimal health care, it is important to expand access to insurance and mental health supports, regulate environmental toxins, diversify and train the workforce, and offer culturally responsive care that is aligned to individuals' values and community strengths.

5 Conclusion

The pervasive gaps in opportunity evident across US systems were crafted over centuries through policies and practices that excluded, harmed, and discriminated against various groups of people, including Black, AI/AN, Latine, and other communities of color and people with disabilities, among others. This history affected access to resources and experiences in US American systems for generations of people, and it is further compounded by contemporary inequities that manifest in different ways for different groups. The binding of poverty and racism, whereby exploitation of labor, exclusion from wealth building, and withholding of resources from Black people and other people of color, including now many immigrant communities, was explicit and its effects long lasting, manifesting in large racial wealth gaps and disproportionate rates of poverty seen today. Economic stability and wealth are highly associated with opportunity and outcomes across an array of domains, including health and education. Economic conditions shape children's experiences across the life course and affect the entire family. These histories contribute to and shape children's experience before they are even born, advantaging White, higher income families and disadvantaging all others to varying degrees, through distinct mechanisms, and in different ways – across every domain of life, including health and education. And these conditions compound over time, influencing generation after generation.

Several public and nonpublic programs exist to bridge opportunity gaps, but none is fully scaled, meaning that many children and families continue to lack access to resources and supports needed to remedy and repair past harms and promote future well-being. Many existing programs have racialized roots, and families of color and immigrant families often have more difficulty accessing, and more negative experiences in, these programs. Improving and expanding access for all eligible families to programs that support child health, well-being, and learning, like Head Start, paid family leave, health insurance and quality unbiased health care, and food assistance, could go a long way to ensuring that all children have the resources and conditions they need to thrive – and ultimately to breaking the link between demography and development. Other policies that are not widely scaled, such as financial reparation programs, baby bonds, and universal basic income, also have the potential to make gains in bridging gaps in economic conditions – including, in some cases, improving economic stability and, in others, wealth generation, both of which can impact health and educational outcomes. A recent report published by the National Academies of Science Engineering and Medicine on closing the opportunity gap for children birth to age eight across health and education identifies several policy recommendations (NASEM, 2023). These include expanding access to universal early care and education opportunities, using an expanded quality framework that addresses issues driving opportunity gaps, like adequate funding, healthy and safe facilities, the language of educational instruction, harsh discipline, and the segregation of children with disabilities. The report also identifies several health and mental health recommendations for policy that include increased access to paid family and medical leave and approaches to address social determinants of health (NASEM, 2023).

Indeed, whereas the education system in the United States is considered to be the "great equalizer," a critical review and reflection of the history of US education makes it clear that US ideals have fallen short. Indeed, the present US education system has created and exacerbated persistent inequities for Black, Latine, AI/AN, Asian, and other children and families of color, those who have disabilities, those living in poverty, and others. These inequities manifest in different ways for different groups but often carry a common theme of exclusion: exclusion via harsh discipline practices, exclusion from general education settings for children with disabilities or English learners, exclusion of people of color from curricula and pedagogy, and exclusion of children's home language, cultures, and/or other identities.

Undoubtedly, reimagining and implementing an equitable educational system constitutes a complex and nuanced challenge that warrants comprehensive, multisector solutions at both individual and collective levels. Addressing one area of education, such as the workforce or assessments in silos, will not yield the meaningful changes necessary to overturn or rectify centuries of injustice, inequity, and oppression. However, identifying the roots of educational injustice and striving to change them in concrete, systematic ways are key to making positive, sustainable changes. As a start, educational justice looks like ensuring that young children have access to high-quality early care and education, children with disabilities are served in general classrooms alongside their peers with appropriate accommodations and quality supports, dual language learners receive high-quality bilingual education, children are treated with respect and love – particularly Black children, who have been on the receiving end of bias and harsh discipline for generations – AI/AN children's cultures and languages are preserved, families' voices are valued, child assessments are valid and fair, and the workforce is well qualified and compensated. Improving the US education system cannot be a color, disability-evasive endeavor, but rather must grapple with US history – as uncomfortable as it may be – to repair past harms and build on what we currently understand are equitable approaches to education. We must also center the voices of marginalized communities across each educational sector and co-create solutions. To reimagine the US American educational system as one that serves all its children and youth, equity cannot be an afterthought but rather be the driving force of how we define a proper, quality education in the US democratic, pluralistic society.

Given that marginalization happens through exclusion and forced assimilation, reimagining an equity-focused education system requires placing the groups of children and families who have been historically marginalized at the forefront of educational initiatives and investments. This prioritization starts with collecting and analyzing data that are disaggregated by demographic variables and allow for intersectional analyses (Bornstein, 2017). Data are then analyzed to strategically plan how to offer system-wide supports that are aligned, monitored, and well funded. Once data is collected, policies, research, learning standards, workforce licensure requirements, funding, monitoring, and accountability must be aligned and made a required expectation across educational systems.

Like the education system, the persistence of racialized health inequities reveals the need for policies that directly address and eliminate barriers that limit access to responsive, quality care in communities that have been marginalized. Decades of research indicate that families of color, as well as those living in poverty and those with disabilities, experience inequities in exposure to environmental toxins, uneven access to health insurance and poorer quality, sometimes biased health care, and more experiences with trauma. Combining federal funding, equity-centered policy, and accountability with local decision-making driven by communities has the potential to scale up the changes needed to realize US ideals for health equity. In addition to community-level care, it is important to note that racism and sexism are key drivers of health disparities, particularly those impacting expecting parents and their children in the United States. Making ideological shifts to interrogate and dismantle widely held negative beliefs associated with racism, sexism, and other forms of oppression requires common awareness of both implicit and explicit bias, as well as an honest reckoning with US American history. Universal health care coverage and access to healthy food, with targeted outreach efforts to communities that have been historically marginalized; investing in culturally grounded community-based health efforts, like doula networks; and improving the quality of health care for historically marginalized communities, with a particular focus on combating bias in health care experiences, are all critical to bridging health disparities. Addressing social determinants of health, which have profound impacts on health outcomes and health disparities, is also critical. This can be done through targeted investments to address the diverse array of inequities in opportunity and resources that marginalized communities face across transportation, housing, education, economic stability and mobility, and so on.

Caring for the overall well-being of children in the United States is integral to creating a democratic society where all citizens are valued and treated with the dignity and respect they deserve to reach their fullest potential. Achieving equity for children requires the conditions, opportunities, and supports necessary to achieve this vision. Funding, policy, accountability, and support structures must be aligned across systems to close opportunity gaps and repair past wrongs, ensuring children and families from historically and contemporary marginalized communities receive equitable access to resources and positive and fair experiences within programs, schools, and health systems. At the foundation of this work must be a focus on equity for families that includes intentional policies to support economic well-being, a healthy start for new parents, adequate quality mental health care to mitigate historical and contemporary trauma and stressors, safe communities and stable housing, and the overall conditions families need to thrive and rear thriving children.

References

Acevedo-Garcia, D. (2003). Future directions in residential segregation and health research: A multilevel approach. *American Journal of Public Health*, *93*, 215–221. https://doi.org/10.1093/acprof:oso/9780195138382.003.0012

Adair, J. K., Colegrove, K. S. S., & McManus, M. E. (2017). How the word gap argument negatively impacts young children of Latinx immigrants' conceptualizations of learning. *Harvard Educational Review*, *87*(3), 309–334. https://doi.org/10.17763/1943-5045-87.3.309

Adams, J. D. (2022). Manifesting Black joy in science learning. *Cultural Studies of Science Education*, *17*(1), 199–209. https://doi.org/10.1007/s11422-022-10114-7

Administration for Children and Families. (2019). Child development and school readiness. In Brief. https://homvee.acf.hhs.gov/outcomes/child%20development%20and%20school%20readiness/In%20brief

Albritton, K., Mathews, R. E., & Anhalt, K. (2019). Systematic review of early childhood mental health consultation: Implications for improving preschool discipline disproportionality. *Journal of Educational and Psychological Consultation*, *29*(4), 444–472. https://doi.org/10.1080/10474412.2018.1541413

Alegria, M., Canino, G., Ríos, R., et al. (2002). Mental health care for Latinos: Inequalities in use of specialty mental health services among Latinos, African Americans, and non-Latino Whites. *Psychiatric Services*, *53*(12), 1547–1555. https://doi.org/10.1176/appi.ps.53.12.1547

Alker, J., & Corcoran, A. (2020). Children's uninsured rate rises by largest annual jump in more than a decade. Georgetown Center for Children and Families. https://ccf.georgetown.edu/2020/10/08/childrens-uninsured-rate-rises-by-largest-annual-jump-in-more-than-a-decade-2/

Almond, D., Hoynes, H. W., & Schanzenbach, D. W. (2011). Inside the war on poverty: The impact of food stamps on birth outcomes. *The Review of Economics and Statistics*, *93*(2), 387–403. https://doi.org/10.1162/REST_a_0008

American Academy of Pediatrics. (2021). Declaration of a national emergency in child and adolescent mental health. www.aap.org/en/advocacy/child-and-adolescent-healthy-mental-development/aap-aacap-cha-declaration-of-a-national-emergency-in-child-and-adolescent-mental-health/

American College of Obstetricians and Gynecologists. (2022). Racism in obstetrics and gynecology: Statement of policy. www.acog.org/clinical-infor

mation/policy-and-position-statements/statements-of-policy/2022/racism-in-obstetrics-gynecology

American Psychological Association. (2012). *Ethnicity and health in America series*. www.apa.org/pi/oema/resources/ethnicity-health

Ansell, D. A., & McDonald, E. K. (2015). Bias, black lives, and academic medicine. *New England Journal of Medicine, 372*(12), 1087–1089. https://doi.org/10.1056/NEJMp1500832

Apelberg, B. J., Buckley, T. J., & White, R. H. (2005). Socioeconomic and racial disparities in cancer risk from air toxics in Maryland. *Environmental Health Perspectives, 113*(6), 693–699. https://doi.org/10.1289/ehp.7609

Aronson, B., & Laughter, J. (2016). The theory and practice of culturally relevant education: Synthesis of research across content areas. *Review of Educational Research, 86*(1), 163–206. https://doi.org/10.3102/0034654315582066

Around Him, D., & Sauyaq Jean Gordon, H. (2022, November). Latest census estimates show disproportionate poverty among American Indian and Alaska Native (AIAN) children and overall AIAN population. Child Trends. https://childtrends.org/blog/latest-census-estimates-show-disproportionate-poverty-among-american-indian-and-alaska-native-aian-children-and-the-overall-aian-population

Artiga, S., & Hinton, E. (2022a). Beyond health care: The role of social determinants in promoting health and health equity. Kaiser Family Foundation. www.kff.org/racial-equity-and-health-policy/issue-brief/beyond-health-care-the-role-of-social-determinants-in-promoting-health-and-health-equity/

Artiga, S., Hill, L., Damico, A. (2022b). Health care coverage by race and ethnicity, 2020–2021. www.kff.org/racial-equity-and-health-policy/issue-brief/health-coverage-by-race-and-ethnicity/

Artiles, A. J. (2019). Fourteenth annual Brown lecture in education research: Reenvisioning equity research: Disability identification disparities as a case in point. *Educational Researcher, 48*(6), 325–335. https://doi.org/10.3102/0013189X19871949

Artiles, A. J., Dorn, S., & Bal, A. (2016). Objects of protection, enduring nodes of difference: Disability intersections with "other" differences, 1916 to 2016. *Review of Research in Education, 40*(1), 777–820. https://doi.org/10.3102/0091732X16680606

Artiles, A. J., & Kozleski, E. B. (2007). Beyond convictions: Interrogating culture, history, and power in inclusive education. *Language Arts, 84*(4), 357–364.

Austin, A., Herrick, H., Proescholdbell, S., & Simmons, J. (2016). Disability and exposure to high levels of adverse childhood experiences: Effect on health and risk behavior. *North Carolina Medical Journal, 77*(1), 30–36. https://doi.org/10.18043/ncm.77.1.30

Avalos, B. (2011). Teacher professional development in teaching and teacher education over ten years. *Teaching and Teacher Education, 27*(1), 10–20. https://doi.org/10.1016/j.tate.2010.08.007

Avramidis, E., & Norwich, B. (2002). Teachers' attitudes towards integration/ inclusion: A review of the literature. *European Journal of Special Needs Education, 17*(2), 129–147. https://doi.org/10.1080/08856250210129056

Barbosa-Leiker, C., Smith, C. L., Crespi, E. J., et al. (2021). Stressors, coping, and resources needed during the COVID-19 pandemic in a sample of peri-natal women. *BMC Pregnancy and Childbirth, 21*(1), 1–13. https://doi.org/10.1186/s12884-021-03665-0

Barnett, W. S., & Frede, E. (2010). The promise of preschool: Why we need early education for all. *US American Educator, 34*(1), 21–40.

Barnett, W. S., Lamy, C., & Jung, K. (2005). The effects of state prekindergarten programs on young children's school readiness in five states. National Institute for Early Education Research. https://citeseerx.ist.psu.edu/document? repid=rep1type=pdf&doi=03a679cecf9c33e758670493f1a1c67e38e8e957

Barnett, W. S., Yarosz, D. J., Thomas, J., et al. (2007). Two-way and monolin-gual English immersion in preschool education: An experimental comparison. *Early Childhood Research Quarterly, 22*(3), 277–293. https://doi.org/10.1016/j.ecresq.2007.03.003

Barton, E. E., & Smith, B. J. (2015). Advancing high-quality preschool inclusion: A discussion and recommendations for the field. *Topics in Early Childhood Special Education, 35*(2), 69–78. https://doi.org/10.1177/0271121415583048

Bates, T. (2006). The urban development potential of black-owned businesses. *Journal of the American Planning Association, 72*(2), 227–237. https://doi.org/10.1080/01944360608976741

Benfer, E. A., & Mohapatra, S. (2020). Health justice strategies to combat the pandemic: Eliminating discrimination, poverty, and health disparities during and after COVID-19. *Yale Journal of Health, Policy, Law, and Ethics, 19,* 122–141. https://openyls.law.yale.edu/bitstream/handle/20.500.13051/5966/ Benfer_v19n3_122_171.pdf?sequence=2

Bernard, D. L., Calhoun, C. D., Banks, D. E., Halliday, C. A., Hughes-Halbert, C., & Danielson, C. K. (2021). Making the "C-ACE" for a culturally-informed adverse childhood experiences framework to understand the perva-sive mental health impact of racism on Black youth. *Journal of Child &*

Adolescent Trauma, *14*, 233–247. https://doi.org/10.1007/s40653-020-00319-9

Bethell, C. D., Davis, M. B., Gombojav, N., et al. (2017). A national and across-state profile on adverse childhood experiences among US children and possibilities to heal and thrive. National Children's Advocacy Center. https://calio.dspacedirect.org/handle/11212/3584

Bialystok, E. (2011). Reshaping the mind: The benefits of bilingualism. Bilingualism as a form of cognitive reserve. *Neurology*, *75*(19), 1726–1729. https://doi.org/10.1037/a002540

Bitsko, R. H., Claussen, A. H., Lichstein, J., et al. (2022). Mental health surveillance among children – United States, 2013–2019. *Morbidity and Mortality Weekly Report Supplements 2022*, *71*(Suppl-2), 1–42. http://doi.org/10.15585/mmwr.su7102a1

Bogan, E., Adams-Bass, V. N., Francis, L. A., et al. (2022). "Wearing a mask won't protect us from our history": The impact of COVID-19 on Black children and families. *Social Policy Report*, *35*(2), 1–33. https://doi.org/10.1002/sop2.23

Bohren, M. A., Hofmeyr, G. J., Sakala, C., et al. (2017). Continuous support for women during childbirth. *The Cochrane Database of Systematic Reviews*, *7*(7), CD003766. https://doi.org/10.1002/14651858.CD003766.pub6

Bonilla-Silva, E. (2021). What makes systemic racism systemic? *Sociological Inquiry*, *91*(3), 513–533. https://doi.org/10.4324/9781003276630-62

Bornstein, M. H. (2017). The specificity principle in acculturation science. *Perspectives on Psychological Science: A Journal of the Association for Psychological Science*, *12*(1), 3–45. https://doi.org/10.1177/174569161665599

Boutakidis, I. P., Chao, R. K., & Rodríguez, J. L. (2011). The role of adolescents' native language fluency on quality of communication and respect for parents in Chinese and Korean immigrant families. *Asian American Journal of Psychology*, *2*(2), 128–139. https://doi.org/10.1037/a0023606

Bowers, V. (2021). Improving access to behavioral health services for racial ethnic minority youth. Center for Health Innovation & Science. https://depts.washington.edu/uwchips/docs/brief-behav-health-youth.pdf

Brooks, F. (2002). Impacts of child care subsidies on family and child well-being. *Early Childhood Research Quarterly*, *17*(4), 498–511. https://doi.org/10.1016/S0885-2006(02)00186-2

Brooks, T., & Gardner, A. (2020). Medicaid and CHIP provide health coverage to more than half of children of color. Georgetown University Health Policy Institute Center for Children and Families. https://ccf.georgetown.edu/2020/

07/27/medicaid-and-chip-provide-health-coverage-to-more-than-half-of-children-of-color/

Bruner, C., & Johnson, K. (2018, March). Developing a public response to improving developmental trajectories and preventing inequities. Center for the Study of Social Policy. https://cssp.org/wp-content/uploads/2018/08/CSSP-Prenatal-to-Three.pdf

Buchanan, L. B., Ward, C. F., & Senta, A. (2021). Deploying Black joy: Learning to teach towards abolition through picture books. In *Handbook of Research on Teaching Diverse Youth Literature to Pre-Service Professionals* (pp. 360–377). IGI Global.

Bucholtz, M., Casillas, D. I., & Lee, J. S. (2017). Language and culture as sustenance. In D. Paris & H. S. Alism (Eds.), *Culturally Sustaining Pedagogies: Teaching and Learning for Justice in a Changing World* (pp. 43–59). Teacher's College Press.

Buss, C., Entringer, S., Moog, N. K., et al. (2017). Intergenerational transmission of maternal childhood maltreatment exposure: Implications for fetal brain development. *Journal of the American Academy of Child & Adolescent Psychiatry, 56*(5), 373–382. https://doi.org/10.1016/j.jaac.2017.03.001

Butler, S. M., Beach, W. W., & Winfree, P. (2008). Pathways to economic stability. Economic Mobility Project. www.pewtrusts.org/~/media/legacy/uploadedfiles/wwwpewtrustsorg/reports/economic_mobility/pewempchartbook12pdf.pdf

Butrica, B. A., & Martinchek, K. (2020, February). Lessons for organizations on effective interventions for economic well-being. Urban Institute. www.urban.org/sites/default/files/publication/101711/LESSON~1_18.PDF

Byrd, N. Z. (2009). The dirty side of domestic work: An underground economy and the exploitation of undocumented workers. *DePaul Journal for Social Justice, 3*, 245–276. https://via.library.depaul.edu/cgi/viewcontent.cgi?article=1058&context=jsj

Caballero, T. M., Johnson, S. B., Buchanan, C. R. M., & DeCamp, L. R. (2017). Adverse childhood experiences among Hispanic children in immigrant families versus US-native families. *Pediatrics, 140* (5), e20170297. https://doi.org/10.1542/peds.2017-0297

Capp, M. J. (2017). The effectiveness of universal design for learning: A meta-analysis of literature between 2013 and 2016. *International Journal of Inclusive Education, 21*(8), 791–807. https://doi.org/10.1080/13603116.2017.1325074

Carruthers, C. K., & Wanamaker, M. H. (2017). Separate and unequal in the labor market: Human capital and the Jim Crow wage gap. *Journal of Labor Economics, 35*(3), 655–696. https://doi.org/10.1086/690944

Castro, D. C., & Meek, S. (2022). Beyond Castañeda and the "language barrier" ideology: Young children and their right to bilingualism. *Language Policy, 21* (3), 407–425. https://doi.org/10.1007/s10993-021-09608-x

Catanzarite, L. (2000). Brown-collar jobs: Occupational segregation and earnings of recent-immigrant Latinos. *Sociological Perspectives, 43*(1), 45–75. https://doi.org/10.2307/1389782

Caughey, A. B., Cahill, A. G., Guise, J. M., et al. (2014). Safe prevention of the primary cesarean delivery. *American Journal of Obstetrics and Gynecology, 210*(3), 179–193. https://doi.org/10.1016/j.ajog.2014.01.026

Center for Applied Special Technology (2023, March). The UDL guidelines. https://udlguidelines.cast.org/?_gl=1*18lrrco*_ga*OTMyMTIyMjk5LjE2ODAyNzA5OTM.*_ga_C7LXP5M74W*MTY4MDI3MDk5Mi4xLjEuMTY4MDI3MTM1MC4wLjAuMA.

Center for the Study of Child Care Employment (2020). Early childhood workforce index 2020: The early childhood educator workforce. https://cscce.berkeley.edu/workforce-index-2020/the-early-educator-workforce/early-educator-pay-economic-insecurity-across-the-state

Centers for Disease Control and Prevention (CDC). (2020). COVID-19 hospitalization and death by race/ethnicity. www.cdc.gov/coronavirus/2019-ncov/covid-data/investigations-discovery/hospitalization-death-by-race-ethnicity.html

Centers for Disease Control and Prevention (CDC). (2022, June). Infant mortality. www.cdc.gov/reproductivehealth/maternalinfanthealth/infantmortality.htm

Center for Disease Control and Prevention (CDC). (2023). *Decreases in young children who received blood lead level testing during COVID-19 – 34 Jurisdictions, January–May 2020.*

Centers for Disease Control and Prevention (CDC). (n.d.). Data and statistics on children's mental health. www.cdc.gov/childrensmentalhealth/data.html

Centers for Medicare and Medicaid Services (2022, April). Medicaid & CHIP enrollment data highlights. www.medicaid.gov/medicaid/program-information/medicaid-and-chip-enrollment-data/report-highlights/index.html

Center of Excellence for Infant and Early Childhood Mental Health Consultation (2023). Promoting Black joy and countering bias through infant and early childhood mental health consultation. www.iecmhc.org/documents/CenteringEquityResource_BlackJoy_FNL.pdf

Center on Poverty & Social Action. (2022, January). 3.7 million more children in poverty in January 2022 without monthly child tax credit. www.povertycenter.columbia.edu/news-internal/monthly-poverty-january-2022

Cheak-Zamora, N. C., & Thullen, M. (2017). Disparities in quality and access to care for children with developmental disabilities and multiple health conditions. *Maternal and Child Health Journal, 21*, 36–44. https://doi.org/10.1007/s10995-016-2091-0

Cheatham, G. A., Santos, R. M., & Kerkutluoglu, A. (2012). Review of comparison studies investigating bilingualism and bilingual instruction for students with disabilities. *Focus on Exceptional Children, 45*(3), 1–12. https://doi.org/10.17161/foec.v45i3.668

Chetty, R., Hendren, N., Jones, M. R., & Porter, S. R. (2020). Race and economic opportunity in in the United States: An intergenerational perspective. *The Quarterly Journal of Economics, 135*(2), 711–783. https://doi.org/10.1093/qje/qjz042

Child Trends (2018). The prevalence of adverse childhood experiences, nationally, by state, and by race or ethnicity. www.childtrends.org/publications/prevalence-adverse-childhood-experiences-nationally-state-race-ethnicity

Christie-Mizell, C. A. (2022). Neighborhood disadvantage and poor health: The consequences of race, gender, and age among young adults. *International Journal of Environmental Research and Public Health, 19*(13), 8107. https://doi.org/10.3390/ijerph19138107

Cholewa, B., Goodman, R. D., West-Olatunji, C., & Amatea, E. (2014). A qualitative examination of the impact of culturally responsive educational practices on the psychological well-being of students of color. *The Urban Review, 46*, 574–596. https://doi.org/10.1007/s11256-014-0272-y

Cioè-Peña, M. (2017). The intersectional gap: How bilingual students in the United States are excluded from inclusion. *International Journal of Inclusive Education, 21*(9), 906–919. https://doi.org/10.1080/13603116.2017.1296032

Civil Rights Data Collection (2021, July). Discipline practices in preschool. https://ocrdata.ed.gov/assets/downloads/crdc-DOE-Discipline-Practices-in-Preschool-part1.pdf

Clark, M., & Burak, E. W. (2022, July). Opportunities to support maternal and child health through Medicaid's new postpartum coverage extension. Georgetown University Center for Children and Families. https://ccf.georgetown.edu/2022/07/15/opportunities-to-support-maternal-and-child-health-through-medicaids-new-postpartum-coverage-extension/

Clement, S., Schauman, O., Graham, T., et al. (2015). What is the impact of mental health-related stigma on help-seeking? A systematic review of quantitative and qualitative studies. *Psychological Medicine, 45*(1), 11–27. https://doi.org/10.1017/S0033291714000129

Coleman, J. S. (1969). Equality of educational opportunity, reexamined. *Socio-economic Planning Sciences, 2*(2–4), 347–354. https://doi.org/10.1016/0038-0121(69)90029-9

Coll, C. G., Crnic, K., Lamberty, G., Wasik, B. H., Jenkins, R., Garcia, H. V., & McAdoo, H. P. (1996). An integrative model for the study of developmental competencies in minority children. *Child Development, 67*(5), 1891–1914. https://doi.org/10.1111/j.1467-8624.1996.tb01834.x

Colón, M., Veloria, C. N., Pica-Smith, C., & Contini, R. M. (2022). A systems analysis of Latine education in Massachusetts: A call for critical intercultural integration. *International Migration*. https://doi.org/10.1111/imig.13099

Congressional Research Service (2019). The Individuals with Disabilities Education Act (IDEA) funding: A primer. https://sgp.fas.org/crs/misc/R44624.pdf

Conners-Burrow, N. A., Whiteside-Mansell, L., Mckelvey, L., Virmani, E. A., & Sockwell, L. (2012). Improved classroom quality and child behavior in an Arkansas early childhood mental health consultation pilot project. *Infant Mental Health Journal, 33*(3), 256–264. https://doi.org/10.1002/imhj.21335

Cornachione, E., Rudowitz, R., & Artiga, A. (2016) Children's health coverage: The role of Medicaid and CHIP and issues for the future. Kaiser Family Foundation. www.kff.org/report-section/childrens-health-coverage-the-role-of-medicaid-and-chip-and-issues-for-the-future-issue-brief/#:~:text=The%20children's%20uninsured%20rate%20has,in%202014%20(Figure%203).&text=This%20decline%20reflects%20expansions%20in,and%20outreach%20and%20enrollment%20campaigns

Courtney, J. G., Chuke, S. O., Dyke, et al. (2021). Decreases in young children who received blood lead level testing during COVID-19 – 34 jurisdictions, January–May 2020. *Morbidity and Mortality Weekly Report, 70*(5), 155.

Coutinho, M. J., Oswald, D. P., & Best, A. M. (2002). The influence of socio-demographics and gender on the disproportionate identification of minority students as having learning disabilities. *Remedial and Special Education, 23*(1), 49–59. https://doi.org/10.1177/074193250202300107

Craik, F. I., Bialystok, E., & Freedman, M. (2010). Delaying the onset of Alzheimer disease: Bilingualism as a form of cognitive reserve. *Neurology, 75*(19), 1726–1729. https://doi.org/10.1212/WNL.0b13e3181fc2a1c

Crenshaw, K. (2013). Demarginalizing the intersection of race and sex: A black feminist critique of antidiscrimination doctrine, feminist theory and antiracist politics. In N. Levit, R. R. M. Vernchick, & M. Minow (Eds.), *Feminist Legal Theories* (pp. 23–51). Routledge.

Cronholm, P. F., Forke, C. M., Wade, R., et al. (2015). Adverse childhood experiences: Expanding the concept of adversity. *American Journal of Preventive Medicine, 49*(3), 354–361. https://doi.org/10.1016/j.amepre.2015.02.001

Cronquist, K., & Lauffer, S. (2019). Characteristics of supplemental nutrition assistance program households: Fiscal year 2017 (No. 9ceac00f7e0f49ef85 d3cc7ebfd2496b). Mathematica Policy Research. www.fns.usda.gov/snap/char acteristics-snap-households-fy-2019

Cushing, I. (2022). Word rich or word poor? Deficit discourses, raciolinguistic ideologies and the resurgence of the 'word gap' in England's education policy. *Critical Inquiry in Language Studies*, 1–27. https://doi-org.ezproxy1 .lib.asu.edu/10.1080/15427587.2022.2102014

Darling-Hammond, L. (2013). Inequality and school resources. In P. L. Carter & K. G. Welner (Eds.), *Closing the Opportunity Gap: What America Must Do to Give Every Child an Even Chance* (pp. 77–97). Oxford University Press.

Daumeyer, N., Onyeador, I., Brown, X., & Richeson, J. (2019). Consequences of attributing discrimination to implicit versus explicit bias. *Journal of Experimental Social Psychology, 84*. https://doi.org/10.1016/j.jesp.2019.04.010.

Davis, A. E., Perry, D. F., & Rabinovitz, L. (2020). Expulsion prevention: Framework for the role of infant and early childhood mental health consultation in addressing implicit biases. *Infant Mental Health Journal, 41*(3), 327–339. https://doi.org/10.1002/imhj.21847

Davis, K., Lillie-Blanton, M., Lyons, B., et al. (1987). Health care for Black Americans: The public sector role. *Milbank Quarterly, 65*, 213–247.

Dee, T. S., & Penner, E. K. (2017). The causal effects of cultural relevance: Evidence from an ethnic studies curriculum. *American Educational Research Journal, 54*(1), 127–166. https://doi.org/10.3102/0002831216677002

Department of Education. (2021). Supporting child and student social, emotional, behavioral, mental health needs. https://www2.ed.gov/documents/ students/supporting-child-student-social-emotional-behavioral-mental-health.pdf

Derenoncourt, E., Kim, C. H., Kuhn, M., & Schularick, M. (2022). Wealth of two nations: The US racial wealth gap, 1860–2020 (No. w30101). National Bureau of Economic Research. https://economics.princeton.edu/working-papers/wealth-of-two-nations-the-u-s-racial-wealth-gap-1860-2020/

Derman-Sparks, L., & Edwards, J. O. (2010). *Anti-bias education for young children and ourselves*. National Association for the Education of Young Children.

Derr, A. S. (2016). Mental health service use among immigrants in the United States: A systematic review. *Psychiatric Services, 67*(3), 265–274. https:// doi.org/10.1176/appi.ps.201500004

Dichter, H., & LiBetti, A. (2021, October). Improving child care compensation backgrounder. The Build Initiative. https://buildinitiative.org/resource-library/backgrounder-on-compensation-in-child-care/

Division for Early Childhood. (2014). DEC recommended practices in early intervention/early childhood special education. www.dec-sped.org/dec-recommended-practices

Dohrmann, K. R., Nishida, T. K., Gartner, A., Lipsky, D. K., & Grimm, K. J. (2007). High school outcomes for students in a public Montessori program. *Journal of Research in Childhood Education*, *22*(2), 205–217. https://doi.org/10.1080/02568540709594622

Dumessa, L., & Kaplan, J. (2022, March 15). Mind the gap: Worsening black maternal mental health outcomes during the pandemic. Adaa.org. https://adaa.org/learn-from-us/from-the-experts/blog-posts/professional/mind-gap-worsening-black-maternal-mental

Dunn, D., & Love, B. L. (2020). Antiracist language arts pedagogy is incomplete without Black joy. *Research in the Teaching of English*, *55*(2), 190–192.

Durán, L. K., Roseth, C. J., & Hoffman, P. (2010). An experimental study comparing English-only and transitional bilingual education on Spanish-speaking preschoolers' early literacy development. *Early Childhood Research Quarterly*, *25*(2), 207–217. https://doi.org/10.1016/j.ecresq.2009.10.002

Earnshaw, V. A., Rosenthal, L., Lewis, J. B., et al. (2013). Maternal experiences with everyday discrimination and infant birth weight: a test of mediators and moderators among young, urban women of color. *Annals of Behavioral Medicine: A Publication of the Society of Behavioral Medicine*, *45*(1), 13–23. https://doi.org/10.1007/s12160-012-9404-3

Education Trust (2022a). Equity across the US and within each state. https://files.eric.ed.gov/fulltext/ED587198.pdf

Education Trust (2022b). School districts that serve students of color receive significantly less funding. https://edtrust.org/press-release/school-districts-that-serve-students-of-color-receive-significantly-less-funding/#:~:text=Across%20the%20country%2C%20districts%20with%20the%20most%20students%20of%20color,for%20a%205%2C000%2Dstudent%20district

Elharake, J. A., Shafiq, M., Cobanoglu, A., et al. (2022). Prevalence of chronic diseases, depression, and stress among US childcare professionals during the COVID-19 pandemic. *Preventing Chronic Disease*, *19*(220132). https://doi.org/10.5888/pcd19.220132

Ely, D. M., & Driscoll, A. K. (2021). Infant mortality in the United States, 2019: Data from the period linked birth/infant death file. National Vital Statistics

Reports: From the Centers for Disease Control and Prevention, National Center for Health Statistics. *National Vital Statistics Reports: From the Centers for Disease Control and Prevention, 70*(14), 1–18.

Emerson, E., Madden, R., Graham, H., et al. (2011). The health of disabled people and the social determinants of health. *Public Health, 125*(3), 145–147. https://doi.org/10.1016/j.puhe.2010.11.003

Eneriz-Wiemer, M., Sanders, L. M., Barr, D. A., & Mendoza, F. S. (2014). Parental limited English proficiency and health outcomes for children with special health care needs: A systematic review. *Academic Pediatrics, 14*(2), 128–136. https://doi.org/10.1016/j.acap.2013.10.003

Epstein, R., Blake, J., & González, T. (2017). Girlhood interrupted: The erasure of Black girls' childhood. Georgetown Law Center on Gender Justice & Opportunity. https://genderjusticeandopportunity.georgetown.edu/wp-con tent/uploads/2020/06/girlhood-interrupted.pdf

Escayg, K. A. (2020). Anti-racism in US early childhood education: Foundational principles. *Sociology Compass, 14*(4), 1–15. https://doi.org/ 10.1111/soc4.12764

Farkas, G. (2003). Racial disparities and discrimination in education: What do we know, how do we know it, and what do we need to know?. *Teachers College Record, 105*(6), 1119–1146. https://doi.org/10.1111/1467-9620.00279

Feagin, J., & Bennefield, Z. (2014). Systemic racism and US health care. *Social Science & Medicine, 103*, 7–14. https://doi.org/10.1016/j.socscimed.2013 .09.006

Felitti, V. J., Anda, R. F., Nordenberg, D., et al. (1998). Relationship of childhood abuse and household dysfunction to many of the leading causes of death in adults: The Adverse Childhood Experiences (ACE) Study. *American Journal of Preventive Medicine, 14*(4), 245–258. https://doi.org/ 10.1016/s0749-3797(98)00017-8

Fiechtner, L., Kleinman, K., Melly, S. J., et al. (2016). Effects of proximity to supermarkets on a randomized trial studying interventions for obesity. *American Journal of Public Health, 106*(3), 557–562. https://doi.org/ 10.2105/AJPH.2015.302986

Fináncz, J., Nyitrai, Á., Podráczky, J., & Csima, M. (2020). Connections between professional well-being and mental health of early childhood educators. *International Journal of Instruction, 13*(4), 731–746. https:// 10.29333/iji.2020.13445a

First Five Years Fund (2021). Child Care and Development Block Grant. www .ffyf.org/issues/ccdbg/#:~:text=Following%20passage%20of%20an% 20FY2018,of%20%245.911%20billion%20in%20FY2021

Fisher, D., Roach, V., & Frey, N. (2002). Examining the general programmatic benefits of inclusive schools. *International Journal of Inclusive Education, 6* (1), 63–78. https://doi.org/10.1080/13603110010035843

FitzGerald, C., & Hurst, S. (2017). Implicit bias in healthcare professionals: A systematic review. *BMC Medical Ethics, 18*(1), 1–18. https://doi.org/10.1186/s12910-017-0179-8

Flores, G., (2010). Racial and ethnic disparities in the health and health care of children. *Pediatrics, 125*(4), e979–e1020. https://doi.org/10.1542/peds.2010-0188

Flores, N., & Rosa, J. (2015). Undoing appropriateness: Raciolinguistic ideologies and language diversity in education. *Harvard Educational Review, 85* (2), 149–171. https://doi.org/10.17763/0017-8055.85.2

Flynn, A. (2023). Black minds matter: A longitudinal analysis of the persistent underrepresentation of Black students in gifted education programs. *Journal for Leadership, Equity, and Research, 9*(1), 6–20.

Ford, D. Y. (2021). *Recruiting and Retaining Culturally Different Students in Gifted Education.* Routledge.

Ford, D. Y., Grantham, T. C., & Whiting, G. W. (2008). Another look at the achievement gap: Learning from the experiences of gifted Black students. *Urban Education, 43*(2), 216–239. https://doi.org/10.1177/00420859073123

Frankenberg, E., E., J., Ayscue, J. B., & Orfield, G. (2019). Harming our common future: America's segregated schools 65 years after *Brown*. The Civil Rights Project. https://escholarship.org/uc/item/23j1b9nv

Freddie Mac. (2022). Racial & ethnic valuation gaps in home purchase appraisals: A modeling approach. www.freddiemac.com/research/insight/20220510-racial-ethnic-valuation-gaps-home-purchase-appraisals-modelingapproach#:~:text=Notably%2C%20the%20pre%2Dmodeling%20appraisal,5.2%25%20in%20the%20AEI%20analysis

Freire, P. (1970). *Pedagogy of the Oppressed.* Seabury Press.

Fuchs, W. W. (2010). Examining teachers' perceived barriers associated with inclusion. *SRATE Journal, 19*(1), 30–35.

Funk, C., & Lopez, M. (2022, June 14). *Hispanic Americans' trust in and engagement with science.* Pew Research Center Science & Society. www.pewresearch.org/science/2022/06/14/a-brief-statistical-portrait-of-u-s-hispanics/

Gallegos, D., Eivers, A., Sondergeld, P., & Pattinson, C. (2021). Food insecurity and child development: A state-of-the-art review. *International Journal of Environmental Research and Public Health, 18*(17), 8990. https://doi.org/10.3390/ijerph18178990

Gándara, P. (2015). The implications of deeper learning for adolescent immigrants and English language learners. Students at the Center: Deeper Learning Research Series. Jobs for the Future. Brooking Institutes.

Gándara, P., & Orfield, G. (2012). Segregating Arizona's English learners: A return to the "Mexican room"? *Teachers College Record, 114*(9), 1–27. https://doi.org/10.1177/016146811211400905

Gardner-Neblett, N., Iruka, I. U., & Humphries, M. (2023). Dismantling the Black–White achievement gap paradigm: Why and how we need to focus instead on systemic change. *Journal of Education, 203*(2), 433–441. https://doi.org/10.1177/00220574211031958

Garfield, R., Damico, A., & Orgera, K. (2020). The coverage gap: Uninsured poor adults in states that do not expand Medicaid. Peterson KFF-Health System Tracker. *Disponível em: Acesso em, 29*, 1–11.

Garver, R., & Hopkins, M. (2020). Segregation and integration in the education of English learners: Leadership and policy dilemmas. *Leadership and Policy in Schools, 19*(1), 1–5. https://doi.org/10.1080/15700763.2019.1711133

Gase, L. N., DeFosset, A. R., Smith, L. V., & Kuo, T. (2014). The association between self-reported grocery store access, fruit and vegetable intake, sugar-sweetened beverage consumption, and obesity in a racially diverse, low-income population. *Frontiers in Public Health, 2*, 229. https://doi.org/10.3389/fpubh.2014.00229

Gay, G. (2000). *Culturally Responsive Teaching: Theory, Research, and Practice*. Teachers College Press.

Geary, C. (2022, March 1). *College pays off. But by how much depends on race, gender, and type of degree*. New America. www.newamerica.org/education-policy/edcentral/college-pays-off/

Gee, G. C., & Payne-Sturges, D. C. (2004). Environmental health disparities: A framework integrating psychosocial and environmental concepts. *Environmental Health Perspectives, 112*(17), 1645–1653. https://doi.org/10.1289/ehp.7074.

Georgetown University Health Policy Institute: Center for Children and Families (2018). Snapshot of children's coverage by race and ethnicity. https://ccf.georgetown.edu/wp-content/uploads/2018/05/Kids-coverage-by-race-ethnicity-update-v2.pdf

Geronimus, A. T. (1992). The weathering hypothesis and the health of African-American women and infants: evidence and speculations. *Ethnicity & Disease, 2*(3), 207–221.

Geronimus, A. T., Hicken, M., Keene, D., & Bound, J. (2006). "Weathering" and age patterns of allostatic load scores among Blacks and Whites in the United States. *American Journal of Public Health, 96*(5), 826–833.

Giano, Z., Wheeler, D. L. & Hubach, R. D. (2020). The frequencies and disparities of adverse childhood experiences in the U.S. *BMC Public Health, 20,* 1327. https://doi.org/10.1186/s12889-020-09411-z

Giles, M. S. (2006). Special focus: Dr. Anna Julia Cooper, 1858–1964: Teacher, scholar, and timeless womanist. *The Journal of Negro Education, 75*(4), 621–634. https://doi.org/10.4135/9781412964517.n92

Gilliam, W. S., Maupin, A. N., Reyes, C. R., et al. (2016). Do early educators' implicit biases regarding sex and race relate to behavior expectations and recommendations of preschool expulsions and suspensions. *Yale University Child Study Center, 9*(28), 1–16.

Gilliam, W. S., & Shahar, G. (2006). Preschool and child care expulsion and suspension: Rates and predictors in one state. *Infants & Young Children, 19*(3), 228–245. https://doi.org/10.1097/00001163-200607000-00007

Gillispie, C. (2019, November). *Young learners, missed opportunities.* The Education Trust. https://edtrust.org/resource/young-learners-missed-opportunities/

Giurgescu, C., McFarlin, B. L., Lomax, J., et al. (2011). Racial discrimination and the Black–White gap in adverse birth outcomes: A review. *Journal of Midwifery & Women's Health, 56*(4), 362–370. https://doi.org/10.1111/j.1542-2011.2011.00034.x

Glantz, A., & Martinez, E. (2018, February 15). For people of color, banks are shutting the door to homeownership. Reveal: The Center for Investigative Reporting. https://revealnews.org/article/for-people-of-color-banks-are-shutting-the-door-to-homeownership/

Goff, P. A., Jackson, M. C., Di Leone, B. A. L., et al. (2014). The essence of innocence: Consequences of dehumanizing Black children. *Journal of Personality and Social Psychology, 106*(4), 526–545. https://doi.org/10.1037/a0035663

Goodman, L. A., Pugach, M., Skolnik, A., & Smith, L. (2013). Poverty and mental health practice: Within and beyond the 50-minute hour: Poverty and mental health practice. *Journal of Clinical Psychology, 69*(2), 182–190. https://doi.org/10.1002/jclp.21957

Goodman, A., & Sianesi, B. (2005). Early education and children's outcomes: How long do the impacts last? *Fiscal Studies, 26*(4), 513–548. https://doi.org/10.1111/j.1475-5890.2005.00022.x

Government Accountability Office (2022, December). Women in the workforce: The gender pay gap is greater for certain racial and ethnic groups and varies by education level. www.gao.gov/products/gao-23-106041

Graham G. (2021). Addressing the disproportionate impact of COVID-19 on communities of color. *Journal of Racial and Ethnic Health Disparities*, *8*(2), 280–282. https://doi.org/10.1007/s40615-021-00989-7

Greenwood, B. N., Hardeman, R. R., Huang, L., & Sojourner, A. (2020). Physician–patient racial concordance and disparities in birthing mortality for newborns. *Proceedings of the National Academy of Sciences of the United States of America*, *117*(35), 21194–21200. https://doi.org/10.1073/pnas.1913405117

Greenwood, C. R., Carta, J. J., Walker, D., et al. (2017). Conceptualizing a public health prevention intervention for bridging the 30 million word gap. *Clinical Child and Family Psychology Review*, *20*, 3–24. https://doi-org.ezproxy1.lib.asu.edu/10.1007/s10567-017-0223-8

Greenwood, C. R., Schnitz, A. G., Carta, J. J., Wallisch, A., & Irvin, D. W. (2020). A systematic review of language intervention research with low-income families: A word gap prevention perspective. *Early Childhood Research Quarterly*, *50*, 230–245. https://doi.org/10.1016/j.ecresq.2019.04.001

Growe, R., & Montgomery, P. S. (2003). Educational equity in America: Is education the great equalizer? *Professional Educator*, *25*(2), 23–29.

Gruber, K. J., Cupito, S. H., & Dobson, C. F. (2013). Impact of doulas on healthy birth outcomes. *The Journal of Perinatal Education*, *22*(1), 49–58. https://doi.org/10.1891/1058-1243.22.1.49

Guiberson, M. (2013). Bilingual myth-busters series language confusion in bilingual children. *Perspectives on Communication Disorders and Sciences in Culturally and Linguistically Diverse (CLD) Populations*, *20*(1), 5–14.

Gunja, M. Z., & Collins, S. R. (2019). Who are the remaining uninsured, and why do they lack coverage. The Commonwealth Fund. www.commonwealth fund.org/publications/issue-briefs/2019/aug/who-are-remaining-uninsured-and-why-do-they-lack-coverage

Hajat, A., MacLehose, R. F., Rosofsky, A., et al. (2021). Confounding by socioeconomic status in epidemiological studies of air pollution and health: Challenges and opportunities. *Environmental Health Perspectives*, *129*(6), 65001. https://doi.org/10.1289/EHP7980

Hall, W. J., Chapman, M. V., Lee, K. M., et al. (2015). Implicit racial/ethnic bias among health care professionals and its influence on health care outcomes: A systematic review. *American Journal of Public Health*, *105*(12), e60–76. https://doi.org/10.2105/AJPH.2015.302903

Hamilton, B. E., Hoyert, D. L., Martin, J. A., et al. (2013). Annual summary of vital statistics: 2010–2011. *Pediatrics*, *131*(3), 548–558. DOI: 10.1542/peds.2012-3769

Hardy, E., Joshi, P., Geronimo, K., et al. (2020, January). Data-for-equity research brief: Unequal availability of Head Start: How neighborhood matters. www.diversitydatakids.org/sites/default/files/2020-01/ddk_unequal-availability-of-head-start_2020_4.pdf

Hart, B., & Risley, T. R. (1995). *Meaningful Differences in the Everyday Experience of Young U.S. American Children*. Paul H. Brookes Publishing.

Hasan, S., & Kumar, A. (2019). Digitization and divergence: Online school ratings and segregation in America. https://cdn.vox-cdn.com/uploads/choru s_asset/file/19931447/Digitization_and_Divergence__Paper__2.pdf

Hayward, B., & Williams, H. A. (2007). Self-taught: African American education in slavery and freedom. *The Journal of Southern History*, *73*(4), 929–930. https://doi.org/10.2307/27649617

HealthyChildren.Org. (2021). Mental health during COVID-19: Signs your child may need more. www.healthychildren.org/English/health-issues/condi tions/COVID-19/Pages/Signs-your-Teen-May-Need-More-Support.asp

Heard-Garris, N., Boyd, R., Kan, K., et al. (2021). Structuring poverty: How racism shapes child poverty and child and adolescent health. *Academic Pediatrics*, *21*(8S), S108–S116. https://doi.org/10.1016/j.acap .2021.05.026

Hemmeter, M. L., Barton, E., Fox, L., et al. (2022). Program-wide implementation of the Pyramid Model: Supporting fidelity at the program and classroom levels. *Early Childhood Research Quarterly*, *59*, 56–73. https://doi.org/ 10.1016/j.ecresq.2021.10.003

Hemmeter, M. L., Fox, L., Snyder, P., et al. (2021). Corollary child outcomes from the Pyramid Model professional development intervention efficacy trial. *Early Childhood Research Quarterly*, *54*, 204–218. https://doi.org/ 10.1016/j.ecresq.2020.08.004

Henderson, S., & Wells, R. (2021). Environmental racism and the contamination of black lives: A literature review. *Journal of African American Studies*, *25*(1), 134–151. https://doi.org/10.1007/s12111-020-09511-5

Hodgkinson, S., Godoy, L., Beers, L. S., et al. (2017). Improving mental health access for low-income children and families in the primary care setting. *Pediatrics*, *139*(1), e20151175.

Hodgson, J. (2022). The transnational defence of Mexican American children's rights in depression-era California. *Comparative American Studies: An International Journal*, *19*(2–3), 165–181. https://doi.org/10.1080/ 14775700.2022.2128247

Hoffman, K. M., Trawalter, S., Axt, J. R., & Oliver, M. N. (2016). Racial bias in pain assessment and treatment recommendations, and false beliefs about biological differences between Blacks and Whites. *Proceedings of the*

National Academy of Sciences, 113(16), 4296–4301.https://doi.org/10.1073/pnas.1516047113

Holzman, C., Eyster, J., Kleyn, M., et al. (2009). Maternal weathering and risk of preterm delivery. *American Journal of Public Health, 99*(10), 1864–1871. https://doi.org/10.2105/AJPH.2008.151589

Homan, P. (2019). Structural sexism and health in the United States: A new perspective on health inequality and the gender system. *American Sociological Review, 84*(3), 486–516. https://doi.org/10.1177/0003122419848723

Hong, Y. S., & Henly, J. R. (2020). Supplemental nutrition assistance program and school readiness skills. *Children and Youth Services Review, 114* (105034), 1–14. https://doi.org/10.1016/j.childyouth.2020.105034

Horan, H., Cheyney, M., Piovanetti, Y., et al. (2021). La crisis de la atención de maternidad: Experts' perspectives on the syndemic of poor perinatal health outcomes in Puerto Rico. *Human Organization, 80*(1), 2–16. https://doi.org/10.17730/1938-3525-80.1.2

Horowitz Menasce J., Igielnik, R., & Kochar, R. (2020). Most U.S. Americans say there is too much economic inequality in the U.S., but fewer than half call it a top priority. Pew Research Center. www.pewresearch.org/social-trends/2020/01/09/trends-in-income-and-wealth-inequality/

Howell, E., & McFeeters, J. (2008). Children's mental health care: Differences by race/ethnicity in urban/rural areas. *Journal of Health Care for the Poor and Underserved, 19*(1), 237–247. https://doi.org/10.1353/hpu.2008.0008

Hoyert, D. L. (2023). Maternal mortality rates in the United States, 2021. NCHS Health E-Stats. https://www2.ed.gov/programs/osepidea/618-data/state-level-data-files/index.html

Hughes, K., Bellis, M. A., Hardcastle, K. A., et al. (2017). The effect of multiple adverse childhood experiences on health: a systematic review and meta-analysis. *The Lancet: Public Health, 2*(8), e356–e366. https://doi.org/10.1016/s2468-2667(17)30118-4

Hung, P., Henning-Smith, C. E., Casey, M. M., et al. (2017). Access to obstetric services in rural counties still declining, with 9 percent losing services, 2004–14. *Health Affairs (Project Hope), 36*(9), 1663–1671. https://doi.org/10.1377/hlthaff.2017.0338

Institute of Medicine Committee on Health Insurance Status and Its Consequences. (2009). America's uninsured crisis: Consequences for health and health care. National Academies Press. https://pubmed.ncbi.nlm.nih.gov/25009923/

Iruka, I. U. (2022). Delivering on the promise of early childhood education for black children: An equity strategy. *New Directions for Child and Adolescent Development, 2022*(183–184), 27–45. https://doi.org/10.1002/cad.20483

Iruka, I. U., Curenton, S. M., Durden, T. R., et al. (2020). *Don't Look Away: Embracing Anti-bias Classrooms*. Gryphon House.

Iruka, I. U., Gardner-Neblett, N., Telfer, N. A., et al. (2022). Effects of racism on child development: Advancing antiracist developmental science. *Annual Review of Developmental Psychology, 4*, 109–132. https://doi.org/10.1146/annurev-devpsych-121020-031339

Johnson, A. D., Ryan, R. M., & Brooks-Gunn, J. (2012). Child-care subsidies: Do they impact the quality of care children experience?: Child-care subsidies and child-care quality. *Child Development, 83*(4), 1444–1461. https://doi.org/10.1111/j.1467-8624.2012.1780.x

Joseph, J. (2020). There's something wrong Here: African-American pregnant women and their babies are at greatest risk in the USA. In B. A. Daviss & R. Davis-Floyd (Eds.), *Birthing Models on the Human Rights Frontier* (pp. 131–144). Routledge.

Kagan, S. L. (2009). American early childhood education: Preventing or perpetuating inequity. *Research Review, 3*, 1–40.

Kaiser Family Foundation (2019). Employer-sponsored coverage rates for the nonelderly by race/ethnicity. www.kff.org/other/stateindicator/nonelderly-employer-coverage-rate-by-raceethnicity/?currentTimeframe=0&sortModel=%7B%22colId%22:%22Location%22,%22sort%22:%22asc%22%7D

Kaiser Family Foundation (2023, March). Status of state Medicaid expansion decisions: Interactive map. www.kff.org/medicaid/issue-brief/status-of-state-medicaid-expansion-decisions-interactive-map/

Kataoka, S. H., Zhang, L., & Wells, K. B. (2002). Unmet need for mental health care among US children: Variation by ethnicity and insurance status. *American Journal of Psychiatry, 159*(9), 1548–1555.

Ke, J., & Ford-Jones, E. L. (2015). Food insecurity and hunger: A review of the effects on children's health and behaviour. *Paediatrics & Child Health, 20*(2), 89–91.

Keefe, R. H., Brownstein-Evans, C., & Polmanteer, R. S. R. (2018). The challenges of idealized mothering: Marginalized mothers living with postpartum. *Affilia, 33*(2), 221–235. https://doi.org/10.1177/0886109917747634

Kendi, I. X. (2022). *How to Be an Antiracist*. One world.

Kessler, R. C., Angermeyer, M., Anthony, J. C., et al. (2007). Lifetime prevalence and age-of-onset distributions of mental disorders in the World Health Organization's World Mental Health Survey Initiative. *World Psychiatry, 6*(3), 168–176.

Kids Matter Inc. (2023). Boarding schools and the history of ICWA. www.kidsmatterinc.org/boarding-schools-and-the-history-ofcwa/?gclid=Cjw

KCAiAuaKfBhBtEiwAht6H78cc9hlcQJo5Tw8IyhO3pVkO5pgbDN7MIJsI aCaezjqvGxPXzephKxoCvTIQAvD_BwE

Kinard, T., Gainer, J., Valdez-Gainer, N., Volk, D., & Long, S. (2021). Interrogating the "gold standard": Play-based early childhood education and perpetuating white supremacy. *Theory Into Practice*, *60*(3), 322–332. https://doi.org/10.1080/00405841.2021.1911587

King, G., Lawm, M., King, S., et al. (2003). A conceptual model of the factors affecting the recreation and leisure participation of children with disabilities. *Physical & Occupational Therapy in Pediatrics*, *23*(1), 63–90. https://doi.org/10.1300/j006v23n01_05

King, L. S., Feddoes, D. E., Kirshenbaum, J. S., et al. (2023). Pregnancy during the pandemic: The impact of COVID-19-related stress on risk for prenatal depression. *Psychological Medicine*, *53*(1), 170–180. https://doi.org/10.1017/S003329172100132X

Kleven, H., Landais, C., & Søgaard, J. E. (2019). Children and gender inequality: Evidence from Denmark. *American Economic Journal: Applied Economics*, *11*(4), 181–209. https://doi.org/10.1257/app.20180010

Kniegge-Tucker, K., Yuma, P., Caplovitz-Barrett, K., et al. (2020). Early childhood mental health consultation: Care providers' experiences of the consultative relationship. *Infant Mental Health Journal*, *41*(4), 563–583. https://doi.org/10.1002/imhj.21865

Knocke, K., Chappel, A., Sugar, S., et al. (2022, December). Doula care and maternal health: An evidence review. Office of Health Policy. https://aspe.hhs.gov/sites/default/files/documents/dfcd768f1caf6fabf3d281f762e8d068/ASPE-Doula-Issue-Brief-12-13-22.pdf

Koegel, L. K., Koegel, R. L., Ashbaugh, K., et al. (2014). The importance of early identification and intervention for children with or at risk for autism spectrum disorders. *International Journal of Speech-Language Pathology*, *16*(1), 50–56. https://doi.org/10.3109/17549507.2013.861511

Kreider, A. R., French, B., Aysola, J., et al. (2016). Quality of health insurance coverage and access to care for children in low-income families. *JAMA Pediatrics*, *170*(1), 43–51. https://doi.org/10.1001/jamapediatrics.2015.3028

Kuchirko, Y. (2019). On differences and deficits: A critique of the theoretical and methodological underpinnings of the word gap. *Journal of Early Childhood Literacy*, *19*(4), 533–562. https://doi.org/10.1177/1468798417747029

Kwon, K.-A., Jeon, S., Jeon, L., & Castle, S. (2019). The role of teachers' depressive symptoms in classroom quality and child developmental outcomes in Early Head Start programs. *Learning and Individual Differences*, *747*, 101748. https://doi.org/10.1016/j.lindif.2019.06.002

Lacarte, V. (2022, June). Immigrant children's Medicaid and CHIP access and participation. Migration Policy. www.migrationpolicy.org/sites/default/files/publications/mpi_chip-immigrants-brief_final.pdf

Ladson-Billings, G. (1994). What we can learn from multicultural education research. *Educational Leadership, 51*(8), 22–26.

Ladson-Billings, G. (1998) Just what is critical race theory and what's it doing in a nice field like education? *International Journal of Qualitative Studies in Education, 11*(1), 7–24. https://doi.org/10.1080/095183998236863

Ladson-Billings, G. (2014). Culturally relevant pedagogy 2.0: Aka the remix. *Harvard Educational Review, 84*(1), 74–84.

Lane, K. L., Powers, L., Oakes, W. P., et al. (2020, April). *Universal screening – systematic screening to shape instruction: Lessons learned & practicalities.* Center on PBIS, University of Oregon. https://assets-global.website-files.com/5d3725188825e071f1670246/5eb435206705b2123f3c6b82_Universal%20Screening%202019%20RDQ%20Brief2.pdf

Leko, M. M., & Brownell, M. T. (2009). Crafting quality professional development for special educators: What school leaders should know. *Teaching Exceptional Children, 42*(1), 64–70.

Levy, L. B., & O'Hara, M. W. (2010). Psychotherapeutic interventions for depressed, low-income women: A review of the literature. *Clinical Psychology Review, 30*(8), 934–950. https://doi.org/10.1016/j.cpr.2010.06.006

Lin, A. (2015). Citizenship education in American schools and its role in developing civic engagement: A review of the research. *Educational Review, 67*(1), 35–63. https://doi.org/10.1080/00131911.2013.813440

Linnan, L., Arandia, G., Bateman, L. A., et al. (2017). The health and working conditions of women employed in childcare. *International Journal of Environmental Research and Public Health, 14*(3), 283–297. https://doi.org/10.3390/ijerph14030283

Liptak, G. S., Benzoni, L. B., Mruzek, D. W., et al. (2008). Disparities in diagnosis and access to health services for children with autism: data from the National Survey of Children's Health. *Journal of Developmental & Behavioral Pediatrics, 29*(3), 152–160.https://doi.org/10.1097/dbp.0b013e318165c7a0

Logan, J. A., Justice, L. M., Yumus, M., et al. (2019). When children are not read to at home: The million word gap. *Journal of Developmental & Behavioral Pediatrics, 40*(5), 383–386. https://doi.org/10.1097/DBP.0000000000000657

Lopez, R. (2002). Segregation and black/white differences in exposure to air toxics in 1990. *Environmental Health Perspectives, 110*(Suppl 2), 289–295. https://doi.org/10.1289/ehp.02110s2289

Mabli, J., Ohls, J., Dragoset, L., et al. (2013). Measuring the effect of Supplemental Nutrition Assistance Program (SNAP) participation on food security. Mathematica Policy Research. www.mathematica.org/publications/ measuring-the-effect-of-supplemental-nutrition-assistance-program-snap-participation-on-food-security

MacDorman, M. F., & Mathews, T. J. (2011). Understanding racial and ethnic disparities in US infant mortality rates. National Center for Health Statistics https://stacks.cdc.gov/view/cdc/12375

Manatt, P., & Phillips, L. L. P. (2019, February). Medicaid's role in addressing social determinants of health. Robert Wood Johnson Foundation. www.rwjf .org/en/insights/our-research/2019/02/medicaid-s-role-in-addressing-social-determinants-of-health.html

Mann, A., Whitaker, A., Torres-Gullien, S., et al. (2019). Cops & no counselors: How the lack of school mental health staff is harming students. https://digital commons.unf.edu/cgi/viewcontent.cgi?article=1052&context=facultyshowcase

March of Dimes. (2018). Nowhere to go: Maternity care deserts across the U.S. www.marchofdimes.org/materials/Nowhere_to_Go_Final.pdf

March of Dimes (2023). March of Dimes Peristats. www.marchofdimes.org/ peristats/

Marian, V., & Shook, A. (2012, September). The cognitive benefits of being bilingual. In *Cerebrum: The Dana Forum on Brain Science*. Dana Foundation.

Matthews, T. J., MacDorman, M. F., & Thoma, M. E. (2015, August). Infant mortality statistics from the 2013 period linked birth/infant death data set. *National Vital Statistics Report, 64*(9), 1–30. https://stacks.cdc.gov/view/ cdc/32752

Mccann-Mortimer, P., Augoustinos, M., & Lecouteur, A. (2004). 'Race' and the Human Genome Project: Constructions of scientific legitimacy. *Discourse & Society, 15*(4), 409–432. https://doi.org/10.1177/0957926504043707

McCarthy, E., & Guerin, S. (2022). Family-centred care in early intervention: A systematic review of the processes and outcomes of family-centered care and impacting factors. *Child: Care, Health and Development, 48*(1), 1–32. https://doi.org/10.1111/cch.12901

McCoy, D. C., Yoshikawa, H., Ziol-Guest, K. M., et al. (2017). Impacts of early childhood education on medium- and long-term educational outcomes. *Educational Researcher, 46*(8), 474–487. https://doi.org/10.3102/001318 9X17737739

McDonald, P. (2012). Workplace sexual harassment 30 years on: A review of the literature: Workplace sexual harassment. *International Journal of Management*

Reviews, 14(1), 1–17. https://doi.org/10.1111/j.1468-2370.2011
.00300.x

McIntosh, K., Girvan, E. J., Fairbanks Falcon, S., et al. (2021a). An equity
focused PBIS approach reduces racial inequities in school discipline:
A randomized controlled trial. *School Psychology, 36*(6), 433–444. https://
doi.org/10.1037/spq0000466

McIntosh, K., Girvan, E., McDaniel, S., et al. (2021b). Effects of an equity
focused PIBS approach to school improvement on exclusionary discipline
and school climate. *Preventing School Failure, 65*(4), 354–361. https://doi
.org/10.1080/1045988X.2021.1937027

McIntosh, K., Moss, E., Nunn, R., et al. (2020). *Examining the Black–White
Wealth Gap.* Brookings Institute.

McKinney, C. O., Hahn-Holbrook, J., Chase-Lansdale, P. L., et al. (2016).
Racial and ethnic differences in breastfeeding. *Pediatrics, 138*(2),
e20152388. https://doi.org/10.1542/peds.2015-2388

McLean, C., Whitebook, M., & Roh, E. (2019). *From unlivable wages to just
pay for early educators.* Center for the Study of Child Care Employment.

Meek, S. E., & Gilliam, W. S. (2016). Expulsion and suspension in early
education as matters of social justice and health equity. *NAM Perspectives,
6*(10). https://doi.org/10.31478/201610e

Meek, S., Iruka, I. U., Soto-Boykin, X., et al. (2022). Equity is quality, quality is
equity. Children's Equity Project. https://childandfamilysuccess.asu.edu/
sites/default/files/2022-06/QRIS-report-062122.pdf

Meek, S., Smith, L., Allen, R., et al. (2020). Start with equity: From the early
years to the early grades. Children's Equity Project and Bipartisan Policy
Center. https://childandfamilysuccess.asu.edu/sites/default/files/2020-07/
CEP-report-071520-FINAL.pdf

Mehdipanah, R., Marra, G., Melis, G., et al. (2018). Urban renewal, gentrifica-
tion and health equity: a realist perspective. *European Journal of Public
Health, 28*(2), 243–248. https://doi.org/10.1093/eurpub/ckx202

Mena Araya, A. E. (2020). Critical thinking for civic life in elementary education: Combining storytelling and thinking tools. *Revista Educación, 44*(2),
24–45. https://doi.org/10.15517/revedu.v44i2.39699

Mental Health America (n.d.). Addressing the youth mental health crisis: The
urgent need for more education, services, and support. https://mhanational
.org/addressing-youth-mental-health-crisis-urgent-need-more-education-ser
vices-and-supports

Merrick, M. T., Ford, D. C., Ports, K. A., et al. (2019). Vital signs: Estimated
proportion of adult health problems attributable to adverse childhood experiences and implications for prevention – 25 States, 2015–2017. *Morbidity and*

Mortality Weekly Report, 68(44), 1–14. https://doi.org/10.15585/mmwr.mm6844e1

Miranda, M. L., Kim, D., Reiter, J., et al. (2009). Environmental contributors to the achievement gap. *Neurotoxicology, 30*(6), 1019–1024. https://doi.org/10.1016/j.neuro.2009.07.012

Moll, L.C., Velez-lbanez. C., Greenberg, J., et al. (1990). Community knowledge and classroom practice: Combining resources for literacy instruction (OBEMLA Contract No. 300-87-0131). University of Arizona, College of Education and Bureau of Applied Research in Anthropology. https://files.eric.ed.gov/fulltext/ED341969.pdf

Monk, C., Feng, T., Lee, S., et al. (2016). Distress during pregnancy: Epigenetic regulation of placenta glucocorticoid-related genes and fetal neurobehavior. *The American Journal of Psychiatry, 173*(7), 705–713. https://doi.org/10.1176/appi.ajp.2015.15091171

Morgan, I., & Amerikaner, A. (2018). Funding gaps 2018: An analysis of school funding equity across the US and within each state. *Education Trust.* https://files.eric.ed.gov/fulltext/ED587198.pdf

Morrisey, M. A. (2013). Health insurance in the United States. In G. Dionne (Ed.), *Handbook of Insurance* (pp. 957–995). Springer.

Muhammad, G. E. (2022). Cultivating genius and joy in education through historically responsive literacy. *Language Arts, 99*(3), 195–204.

Muhammad, G. E., Ortiz, N. A., & Neville, M. L. (2021). A historically responsive literacy model for reading and mathematics. *The Reading Teacher, 75*(1), 73–81.

Mydam, J., David, R. J., Rankin, K. M., et al. (2019). Low birth weight among infants born to Black Latina women in the United States. *Maternal and Child Health Journal, 23*(4), 538–546. https://doi.org/10.1007/s10995-018-2669-9

Mykyta, L., Keisler-Starkey, K., & Bunch, L. (2022, September). *More children were covered by Medicaid and CHIP in 2021.* US Census Bureau. www.census.gov/library/stories/2022/09/uninsured-rate-of-children-declines.html

National Academies of Sciences, Engineering, and Medicine. (2019). A roadmap to reducing child poverty. https://nap.nationalacademies.org/catalog/25246/a-roadmap-to-reducing-child-poverty

National Academies of Sciences, Engineering, and Medicine. (2023). Closing the opportunity gap for young children. www.nationalacademies.org/ocga/briefings-to-congress/closing-the-opportunity-gap-for-young-children

National Center for Health Statistics. (2020). Early release of selected mental health estimates based on data from the January–June 2019 National Health

Interview Survey. Center for Disease Control and Prevention. www.cdc.gov/nchs/data/nhis/earlyrelease/ERmentalhealth-508.pdf

National Center for Learning Disabilities (2013). Diplomas at-risk: A critical look at the graduation rate of students with learning disabilities. www.ncld.org/research/diplomas-at-risk-2/

National Center for Learning Disabilities (2021). IDEA full funding: Why should Congress invest in special education? https://ncld.org/news/policy-and-advocacy/idea-full-funding-why-should-congress-invest-in-special-education/

National Conference of State Legislatures (2022). State and federal environmental justice efforts. www.ncsl.org/environment-and-natural-resources/state-and-federal-environmental-justice-efforts

National Health Expenditure Accounts (2021). National health expenditures 2020 highlights. www.cms.gov/Research-Statistics-Data-and-Systems/Statistics-Trends-and-Reports/NationalHealthExpendData/NationalHealthAccountsHistorical

National Home Visiting Resource Center (2021). 2021 home visiting yearbook. https://nhvrc.org/yearbook/2021-yearbook/

National Human Genome Research Institute (2021, November). Eugenics: Its origin and development. www.genome.gov/about-genomics/educational-resources/timelines/eugenics

National Institute for Early Education and Research [NIEER] (2020). The state of preschool 2020. https://nieer.org/wp-content/uploads/2022/09/YB2020_Full_Report.pdf

National Institute for Early Education and Research [NIEER] (2021). The state of preschool 2021. https://nieer.org/wp-content/uploads/2022/09/YB2021_Full_Report.pdf

National Survey of Children with Special Health Care Needs. (2022, February). Cdc.gov. www.cdc.gov/nchs/slaits/cshcn.htm

Nelson, S. L., & Williams, R. O. (2019). From slave codes to educational racism: Urban education policy in the united states as the dispossession, containment, dehumanization, and disenfranchisement of black peoples. *Journal of Law in Society, 19*(1–2), 82–120.

Newacheck, P. W., Hung, Y.-Y., & Wright, K. K. (2002). Racial and ethnic disparities in access to care for children with special health care needs. *Ambulatory Pediatrics: The Official Journal of the Ambulatory Pediatric Association, 2*(4), 247–254. https://doi.org/10.1367/1539-4409(2002)002<0247:raedia>2.0.co;2

Nieto, S. (2000). Placing equity front and center: Some thoughts on transforming teacher education for a new century. *Journal of Teacher Education, 51*(3), 180–187. https://doi.org/10.1177/0022487100051003004

Obinna, D. N. (2021). Confronting disparities: Race, ethnicity, and immigrant status as intersectional determinants in the COVID-19 era. *Health Education & Behavior: The Official Publication of the Society for Public Health Education, 48*(4), 397–403. https://doi.org/10.1177/10901981211011581

O'Brien, R., Neman, T., Seltzer, N., et al. (2020). Structural racism, economic opportunity and racial health disparities: Evidence from US counties. *SSM-Population Health, 11*. https://doi.org/10.1016/j.ssmph.2020.100564

Office of Child Care (2020). Administration of Children and Families. www .acf.hhs.gov/occ/data/fy-2020-preliminary-data-table-12a

Office of Early Childhood Development. (2023, March). *Dear Colleague Letter on Funding to Test for and Address Lead in Water in Early Care and Education Settings.* Administration of Children and Families. www.acf.hhs .gov/sites/default/files/documents/ecd/EPA%20ADM%20Regan%2BHHS %20Sec.%20Becerra%20-%20Lead.pdf

Office of Head Start (2022). Early Head Start Services snapshot national 2020–21. Administration of Children and Families. https://eclkc.ohs .acf.hhs.gov/sites/default/files/pdf/no-search/service-snapshot-ehs-2020- 2021.pdf

Office of Minority Health. (2018). Asthma and African Americans. U.S. Department of Health and Human Services. www.minorityhealth.hhs.gov/ asthma-and-african-americans

Ohri-Vachaspati, P., DeWeese, R. S., Acciai, F., et al. (2019). Healthy food access in low-income high-minority communities: A longitudinal assessment – 2009–2017. *International Journal of Environmental Research and Public Health, 16*(13), 1–14. https://doi.org/10.3390/ijerph16132354

Okonofua, J. A., & Eberhardt, J. L. (2015). Two strikes: Race and the disciplining of young students. *Psychological Science, 26*(5), 617–624. https://doi .org/10.1177/0956797615570365

O'Reggio, M. (2017, February 13). Quality 101: Identifying the core components of a high-quality early childhood program. Center for American Progress. www.Americanprogress.org/article/quality-101-identifying-the- core-components-of-a-high-quality-early-childhood-program/

Orfield, G. (2001). Schools more separate: Consequences of a decade of resegregation. The Civil Rights Project. Harvard University. https://files .eric.ed.gov/fulltext/ED459217.pdf

Osterman, M. J., & Martin, J. A. (2018). SystemTiming and adequacy of prenatal care in the United States, 2016. *National Vital Statistics Report, 67* (3), 1–13. https://stacks.cdc.gov/view/cdc/55174

Padilla, A. M., Chen, X., Swanson, E., et al. (2022). Longitudinal study of Spanish Dual Language Immersion graduates: Secondary school academic and language achievement. *Foreign Language Annals*, *55*(2), 408–434. https://doi.org/10.1111/flan.12615

Panchal, N., Kamal, R., Cox, C., et al. (2021). The implications of COVID-19 for mental health and substance use: An issue brief. www.kff.org/corona virus-covid-19/issue-brief/the-implications-of-covid-19-for-mental-health-and-substance-use/

Pankewicz, A., Davis, R. K., Kim, J., et al. Children with special needs: Social determinants of health and care coordination. *Clinical Pediatrics*, *59*(13), 1161–1168. https://doi.org/10.1177/0009922820941206

Paradise, J. (2014). The impact of Children's Health Insurance Program (CHIP): What does the research tell us? www.kff.org/report-section/the-impact-of-the-childrens-health-insurance-program-chip-issue-brief/

Paris, D. (2012). Culturally sustaining pedagogy: A needed change in stance, terminology, and practice. *Educational Researcher*, *41*(3), 93–97. https://doi.org/10.3102/0013189X12441244

Paris, D., & Alim, H. S. (2014). What are we seeking to sustain through culturally sustaining pedagogy? A loving critique forward. *Harvard Educational Review*, *84*(1), 85–100. https://doi.org/10.17763/haer.84.1.9821873k2ht16m77

Patrick, S. W., Henkhaus, L. E., Zickafoose, J. S., et al. (2020). Well-being of parents and children during the COVID-19 pandemic: A national survey. *Pediatrics*, *146*(4), e2020016824. https://doi.org/10.1542/peds.2020-016824

Pavalko, E. K., Mossakowski, K. N., & Hamilton, V. J. (2003). Does perceived discrimination affect health? Longitudinal relationships between work discrimination and women's physical and emotional health. *Journal of Health and Social Behavior*, *44*(1), 18–33. https://doi.org/10.2307/1519813

Penner, L. A., Dovidio, J. F., West, T. V., et al. (2010). Aversive racism and medical interactions with Black patients: A field study. *Journal of Experimental Social Psychology*, *46*(2), 436–440. https://doi.org/10.1016/j.jesp.2009.11.004

Penner, L. A., Phelan, S. M., Earnshaw, V., et al. (2017). Patient stigma, medical interactions, and health care disparities: A selective review. In B. Major, J. F. Dovidio, & B.G. Link (Eds.), *The Oxford Handbook of Stigma, Discrimination, and Health* (pp. 183–201). Oxford University Press. https://doi.org/10.1093/oxfordhb/9780190243470.001.0001

Perls, H. (2020, November). EPA Undermines its own environmental justice programs. Harvard Environmental & Energy Law Program-EPA Missions Tracker. https://eelp.law.harvard.edu/2020/11/epa-undermines-its-own-environmental-justice-programs/

Perrin, J. M., Lu, M. C., Geller, A., et al. (2020). Vibrant and healthy kids: Aligning science, practice, and policy to advance health equity. *Academic Pediatrics, 20*(2), 160–162. https://doi.org/10.1016/j.acap.2019.11.019

Perry, M. J., Arrington, S., Freisthler, M. S., et al. (2021). Pervasive structural racism in environmental epidemiology. *Environmental Health, 20*, 1–13.

Petersen, E. E., Davis, N. L., Goodman, D., et al. (2019a). Racial/ethnic disparities in pregnancy-related deaths – United States, 2007–2016. *Morbidity and Mortality Weekly Report, 68*(35), 762–765.

Petersen, E. E., Davis, N. L., Goodman, D., et al. (2019b). Vital signs: Pregnancy-related deaths, United States, 2011–2015, and strategies for prevention, 13 states, 2013–2017. *Morbidity and Mortality Weekly Report, 68* (18), 423. http://doi.org/10.15585/mmwr.mm6818e1

Peterson, M. (2016, Fall). IDEA's Impact. Lehigh University. https://ed.lehigh .edu/theory-to-practice/2016/IDEAs-impact#:~:text=Before%20IDEA%2C %20children%20with%20disabilities,no%20access%20to%20public% 20schools

Pitts, J. (2020). What anti-racism really means for educators. Learning for Justice. www.learningforjustice.org/magazine/what-antiracism-really-means-for-educators.

Podgursky, M., & Springer, M. (2011). Teacher compensation systems in the United States K–12 public school system. *National Tax Journal, 64*(1), 165–192. https://doi.org/10.17310/ntj.2011.1.07

Portes, A. (2002). English-only triumphs, but the costs are high. *Contexts, 1*(1), 10–15.

Powell, J. J. (2015). *Barriers to Inclusion: Special Education in the United States and Germany.* Routledge.

Powers, J. M. (2008). Forgotten history: Mexican American school segregation in Arizona from 1900–1951. *Equity & Excellence in Education: University of Massachusetts School of Education Journal, 41*(4), 467–481. https://doi.org/ 10.1080/10665680802400253

Priester, M. A., Browne, T., Iachini, A., et al. (2016). Treatment access barriers and disparities among individuals with co-occurring mental health and substance use disorders: An integrative literature review. *Journal of Substance Abuse Treatment, 61*, 47–59. https://doi.org/10.1016/j.jsat.2015.09.006

Rao, K., Smith, S. J., & Lowrey, K. A. (2017). UDL and intellectual disability: What do we know and where do we go? *Intellectual and Developmental Disabilities, 55*(1), 37–47. https://doi.org/10.1352/1934-9556-55.1.37

Rasmussen, B. (2010). "Attended with great inconveniences": Slave literacy and the 1740 South Carolina Negro Act. *PMLA, 125*(1), 201–203. https://doi .org/10.1632/pmla.2010.125.1.2

Reardon, S. F., & Owens, A. (2014). 60 years after Brown: Trends and consequences of school segregation. *Annual Review of Sociology, 40,* 199–218.

Rhodes, L. (2023). The maternal mental health of Black women. Counseling Today. https://ct.counseling.org/2023/03/the-maternal-mental-health-of-black-women/

Richard, K. (2014). The wealth gap for women of color. Center for Global Policy Solutions. https://digitalcommons.unf.edu/cgi/viewcontent.cgi?article=1052&context=facultyshowcase

Robert Wood Johnson Foundation (2017, September). Mental health & Latino kids. Salud America! https://salud-america.org/wp-content/uploads/2017/09/Issue-Brief-mental-health-9-12-17.Pdf

Rosales, J., & Walker, T. (2021, March). The racist beginnings of standardized testing. National Education Association. www.nea.org/advocating-for-change/new-from-nea/racist-beginnings-standardized-testing

Roth, L. M., & Henley, M. M. (2012). Unequal motherhood: Racial-ethnic and socioeconomic disparities in cesarean sections in the United States. *Social Problems, 59*(2), 207–227. DOI:10.1525/sp.2012.59.2.207

Rothbart, M. W. (2020). Does school finance reform reduce the race gap in school funding? *Education Finance and Policy, 15*(4), 675–707. https://doi.org/10.1162/edfp_a_00282

Rudowitz, R., Garfield, R., & Hinton, E. (2019). 10 things to know about Medicaid: Setting the facts straight. Kaiser Family Foundation. www.kff.org/medicaid/issue-brief/10-things-to-know-about-medicaid-setting-the-facts-straight/#:~:text=Medicaid%20covers%201%20in%205,75%20million%20low%2Dincome%20Americans.

Safon, C. B., McCloskey, L., Ezekwesili, C., et al. (2021). Doula care saves lives, improves equity, and empowers mothers: State Medicaid programs should pay for it. Health Affairs Blog. www.healthaffairs.org/do/10.1377/hblog20210525,295915.

Saluja, B., & Bryant, Z. (2021). How implicit bias contributes to racial disparities in maternal morbidity and mortality in the United States. *Journal of Women's Health* (2002), *30*(2), 270–273. https://doi.org/10.1089/jwh.2020.8874

Sansom, G., & Hannibal, B. (2021). Disparate access to nutritional food: Place, race and equity in the United States. *BMC Nutrition, 7*(1), 1–6. https://doi.org/10.1186/s40795-021-00434-2

Santiago, C. D., Kaltman, S., & Miranda, J. (2013). Poverty and mental health: How do low-income adults and children fare in psychotherapy?: Poverty and mental health. *Journal of Clinical Psychology, 69*(2), 115–126. https://doi.org/10.1002/jclp.21951

Schickedanz, A., Dreyer, B. P., & Halfon, N. (2015). Childhood poverty: Understanding and preventing the adverse impacts of a most-prevalent risk to pediatric health and well-being. *Pediatric Clinics*, *62*(5), 1111–1135. https://doi.org/10.1016/j.pcl.2015.05.008

Schildkamp, K. (2019). Data-based decision-making for school improvement: Research insights and gaps. *Educational Research*, *61*(3), 257–273.

Scholar Institute of Medicine (1999). *Toward Environmental Justice: Research, Education, and Health Policy Needs*. National Academy Press.

Serafini, E. J., Rozell, N., & Winsler, A. (2022). Academic and English language outcomes for DLLs as a function of school bilingual education model: The role of two-way immersion and home language support. *International Journal of Bilingual Education and Bilingualism*, *25*(2), 552–570. https://doi.org/10.1080/13670050.2019.1707477

Shippen, M. E., Crites, S. A., Houchins, D. E., et al. (2005). Preservice teachers' perceptions of including students with disabilities. *Teacher Education and Special Education*, *28*(2), 92–99. https://doi.org/10.1177/088840640502800202

Shivers, E. M., Faragó, F., & Gal-Szabo, D. E. (2022). The role of infant and early childhood mental health consultation in reducing racial and gender relational and discipline disparities between Black and White preschoolers. *Psychology in the Schools*, *59*(10), 1965–1983. https://doi.org/10.1002/pits.22573

Shonkoff, J. P., & Phillips, D. A. (2000). *From Neurons to Neighborhoods: The Science of Early Childhood Development*. National Academies Press.

Silver, H. C., & Zinsser, K. M. (2020). The interplay among early childhood teachers' social and emotional well-being, mental health consultation, and preschool expulsion. *Early Education and Development*, *31*(7), 1133–1150. https://doi.org/10.1080/10409289.2020.1785267

Simmons, D. (2019). How to be an antiracist educator. *ASCD Education Update*, *61*(10), 1–4.

Simons, R. L., Lei, M. K., Beach, S. R., et al. (2016). Economic hardship and biological weathering: the epigenetics of aging in a US sample of black women. *Social Science & Medicine*, *150*, 192–200. https://doi.org/10.1016/j.socscimed.2015.12.001

Skiba, R. J., Michael, R. S., Nardo, A. C., et al. (2002). The color of discipline: Sources of racial and gender disproportionality in school punishment. *The Urban Review*, *34*, 317–342.

Solomon, D., Maxwell, C., & Castro, A. (2019). Systematic inequality and economic opportunity. Center for American Progress. www.Americanprogress.org/article/systematic-inequality-economic-opportunity/

Somerville, K., Neal-Barnett, A., Stadulis, R., et al. (2021). Hair cortisol concentration and perceived chronic stress in low-income urban pregnant and postpartum black women. *Journal of Racial and Ethnic Health Disparities, 8*(2), 519–531. https://doi.org/10.1007/s40615-020-00809-4

Soto-Boykin, X. T., Larson, A. L., Olszewski, A., et al. (2021). Who is centered? A systematic review of early childhood researchers' descriptions of children and caregivers from linguistically minoritized communities. *Topics in Early Childhood Special Education, 41*(1), 18–30. https://doi.org/10.1177/0271121421991222

Spencer, N., Warner, G., Marchi, J., et al. (2022). 'Hidden pandemic': Orphanhood and loss of caregivers in the COVID-19 pandemic. *BMJ Paediatrics Open, 6*(1), e001604. https://doi.org/10.1136/bmjpo-2022-001604

Steele, J. L., Slater, R. O., Li, J., et al. (2018). Dual-language immersion education at scale: An analysis of program costs, mechanisms, and moderators. *Educational Evaluation and Policy Analysis, 40*(3), 420–445. https://doi.org/10.3102/0162373718779457

Strand, N. H., Mariano, E. R., Goree, J. H., et al. (2021, June). Racism in pain medicine: We can and should do more. *Mayo Clinic Proceedings, 96*(6), 1394–1400.

Substance Abuse and Mental Health Services Administration (2020) National survey on drug use and health. www.samhsa.gov/data/release/2020-national-survey-drug-use-and-health-nsduh-releases

Sullivan, J., Wilton, L., & Apfelbaum, E. P. (2021). Adults delay conversations about race because they underestimate children's processing of race. *Journal of Experimental Psychology: General, 150*(2), 1–6. https://doi.org/10.1037/xge0000851

Swope, C. B., Hernández, D., & Cushing, L. J. (2022). The relationship of historical redlining with present-day neighborhood environmental and health outcomes: A scoping review and conceptual model. *Journal of Urban Health, 99*(6), 959–983. https://doi.org/10.1007/s11524-022-00665-z

Syed, S. T., Gerber, B. S., & Sharp, L. K. (2013). Traveling towards disease: Transportation barriers to health care access. *Journal of Community Health, 38*(5), 976–993. https://doi.org/10.1007/s10900-013-9681-1

Tamir, C. (2021). The growing diversity of Black America. The Pew Research Center. www.pewresearch.org/social-trends/2021/03/25/the-growing-diversity-of-black-america/

Taylor, D. (2014). *Toxic Communities: Environmental Racism, Industrial Pollution, and Residential Mobility.* NYU Press.

Taylor, T., & Salyakina, D. (2019). Health care access barriers bring children to emergency rooms more frequently: A representative survey. *Population*

Health Management, 22(3), 262–271. https://doi.org/10.1089/pop.2018
.0089

Tessum, C. W., Paolella, D. A., Chambliss, S. E., et al. (2021). PM2. 5 polluters
disproportionately and systemically affect people of color in the United
States. *Science Advances, 7*(18), 1–6. https://doi.org/10.1126/sciadv.abf4491

Thompson, D. L., & Thompson, S. (2018). Educational equity and quality in K–
12 schools: Meeting the needs of all students. *Journal for the Advancement of
Educational Research International, 12*(1), 34–46.

Treglia, D., Cutuli, J. J., Arasteh, K., et al. (2022). Parental and other caregiver
loss due to COVID-19 in the United States: Prevalence by race, state,
relationship, and child age. *Journal of Community Health, 48*(3), 1–8.
https://doi.org/10.1007/s10900-022-01160-x

Trent, M., Dooley, D. G., Dougé, J., et al. (2019). The impact of racism on child
and adolescent health. *Pediatrics, 144*(2), e20191765. https://doi.org/
10.1542/peds.2019-1765

Trost, S., Beauregard, J., Chandra, G., et al., (2019). Pregnancy-related deaths:
Data from maternal mortality review committees in 36 US states, 2017–2019.
Center for Disease Control. www.cdc.gov/reproductivehealth/maternal-mor
tality/docs/pdf/Pregnancy-Related-Deaths-Data-MMRCs-2017-2019-H.pdf

Trust for Learning (2023). Principles of ideal learning environments. https://
trustforlearning.org/explore-ideal-learning/principles/

Ullrich, R., Schmit, S., & Cosse, R. (2019). Inequitable access to child care
subsidies. The Center for Law and Social Policy. www.clasp.org/publica
tions/report/brief/inequitable-access-child-care-subsidies#:~:text=Inequitable
%20Access%20to%20Child%20Care%20Subsidies%20Child%20care,the
%20Child%20Care%20and%20Development%20Block%20Grant,20.

UnidosUS (2022, July). The looming equity crisis in children's health care:
Federal and state action is needed to prevent millions of children from losing
Medicaid. https://unidosus.org/publications/the-looming-equity-crisis-in-
childrens-health-care/

United Negro Fund (2023). K–12 disparity facts and statistics. https://uncf.org/
pages/k-12-disparity-facts-and-stats

Upshur, C., Wenz-Gross, M., & Reed, G. (2009). A pilot study of early
childhood mental health consultation for children with behavioral problems
in preschool. *Early Childhood Research Quarterly, 24*(1), 29-45. https://doi
.org/10.1016/j.ecresq.2008.12.002

US Bureau of Labor Statistics. (2021). Occupational employment and wages:
39-9011 childcare workers. www.bls.gov/oes/current/oes399011.htm

US Census Bureau (2021, January). Annual Business Survey released provides
data on minority-owned, veteran-owned, and women-owned businesses.

www.census.gov/newsroom/press-releases/2021/annual-business-survey
.html#:~:text=In%202018%2C%20Hispanic%2Downed%20businesses,
%24101.1%20billion%20in%20annual%20payroll

US Census Bureau (2022a). 2020 ACS 5 year: Estimate detailed tables: Poverty status in the past 12 months by sex by age (White alone). https://data.census.gov/cedsci/table?q=poverty%20and%20age%20and%20race%20ethnicity&tid=ACSDT5Y2020.B17001A.

US Census Bureau (2022b). 2020 ACS 5 year: Estimate detailed tables: Poverty status in the past 12 months by sex by age (Black alone). https://data.census.gov/cedsci/table?q=poverty%20and%20age%20and%20race%20ethnicity&tid=ACSDT5Y2020.B17001B

US Census Bureau. (2023). A third of movers from Puerto Rico to the mainland United States relocated to Florida in 2018. www.census.gov/library/stories/2019/09/puerto-rico-outmigration-increases-poverty-declines.html

USDA. (2021). Economic research service using data from US Department of Commerce, Bureau of the Census, 2021 current population survey food security supplement. www.ers.usda.gov/webdocs/DataFiles/50764/techdoc2021.pdf?v=9487

USDA. (2023). Food security status of U.S. Households in 2022. www.ers.usda.gov/topics/food-nutrition-assistance/food-security-in-the-u-s/key-statistics-graphics/#:~:text=In%202022%3A,with%20adults%2C%20were%20food%20insecure

USDA Food Environment Atlas. (2020, September). McKinsey Global Institute for Black Economic Mobility. www.ers.usda.gov/data-products/food-environment-atlas/

US Department of Education. (2020). Civil rights data collection for the year 2017–2018 school year. https://www2.ed.gov/about/offices/list/ocr/docs/crdc-2017-18.html

US Department of Education. (2022a). 43rd annual report to Congress on the implementation of IDEA. https://sites.ed.gov/idea/files/43rd-arc-for-idea.pdf.

US Department of Education. (2022b). IDEA American rescue plan funds. https://www2.ed.gov/policy/speced/leg/arp/index.html

US Department of Education (2022c, November). A History of Individuals with Disabilities Act. Department of Education IDEA. https://sites.ed.gov/idea/IDEA-History

US Department of Education (2023). IDEA section 619 data products: State level data files. https://www2.ed.gov/programs/osepidea/618-data/state-level-data-files/index.html

US Department of Health and Human Services, Administration for Children and Families (1998). Tobacco use among U.S. racial/ethnic minority groups: African Americans, American Indians and Alaska Natives, Asian U.S. Americans and Pacific Islanders, and Hispanics: A report of the Surgeon General. Department of Health and Human Services, Centers for Disease Control and Prevention, National Center for Chronic Disease Prevention and Health Promotion, Office on Smoking and Health. http://www.cdc.gov/tobacco/sgr/sgr_1998/sgr-min-sgr.htm

US Department of Health and Human Services, Administration for Children and Families (2010, January). Head Start impact study: Final report. Washington, DC. https://files.eric.ed.gov/fulltext/ED507845.pdf

Wade Jr, R., Shea, J. A., Rubin, D., et al. (2014). Adverse childhood experiences of low income urban youth. *Pediatrics*, *134*(1), e13–e20.

Walker, D., & Carta, J. J. (2020). Intervention research to improve language-learning opportunities and address the inequities of the word gap. *Early Childhood Research Quarterly*, *50*, 1–5. https://doi.org/10.1016/j.ecresq.2019.10.008

Ward, E., Wiltshire, J. C., Detry, M. A., et al. (2013). African American men and women's attitude toward mental illness, perceptions of stigma, and preferred coping behaviors. *Nursing Research*, *62*(3), 185–194. https://doi.org/10.1097/NNR.0b013e31827bf533

Weathers, E. S., & Sosina, V. E. (2022). Separate remains unequal: Contemporary segregation and racial disparities in school district revenue. *American Educational Research Journal*, *59*(5), 905–938. https://doi.org/10.3102/00028312221079297

Wechsler, M., Melnick, H., Maier, A., et al. (2016). The building blocks of high-quality early childhood education programs (policy brief). Learning Policy Institute. https://learningpolicyinstitute.org/product/building-blocks-high-quality-early-childhood-education-programs?gclid=CjwKCAjwzuqgBhAcEiwAdj5dRs64Ng5mXWjngzATPPHnNB-edX1VFbHZVQD7wNuGz_odcLvmkoAX-RoCNq8QAvD_BwE

Whitaker, R. C., Becker, B. D., Herman, A. N., et al. (2013). The physical and mental health of Head Start staff: The Pennsylvania Head Start staff wellness survey, 2012. *Preventing Chronic Disease*, *10*, E181. https://doi.org/10.5888/pcd10.130171

Wiedeman, C. R. (2002). Teacher preparation, social justice, equity: A review of the literature. *Equity & Excellence in Education: University of Massachusetts School of Education Journal*, *35*(3), 200–211. https://doi.org/10.1080/713845323

Williams, H. A. (2009). *Self-taught: African American Education in Slavery and Freedom.* University of North Carolina Press.

Williams, M. G. (2022). "They never told us that Black is beautiful": Fostering Black joy and pro-Blackness pedagogies in early childhood classrooms. *Journal of Early Childhood Literacy, 22*(3), 357–382. https://doi.org/10.1177/14687984221121163

Willis, A. I. (2022). Black literacy education in the United States. *Oxford Research Encyclopedia of Education.* https://oxfordre.com/education/display/10.1093/acrefore/9780190264093.001.0001/acrefore-9780190264093-e-1751?rskey=ukwXC0&result=1

Wint, K., Elias, T. I., Mendez, G., et al. (2019). Experiences of community doulas working with low-income, African American mothers. *Health Equity, 3*(1), 109–116. https://doi.org/10.1089/heq.2018.0045

Wong, V. C., Cook, T. D., Barnett, W. S., et al. (2008). An effectiveness-based evaluation of five state pre-kindergarten programs. *Journal of Policy Analysis and Management: The Journal of the Association for Public Policy Analysis and Management, 27*(1), 122–154.

Workman, S., & Ullrich, R. (2017, February). Quality 101: Identifying the core components of high-quality early childhood program. Center for American Progress. www.Americanprogress.org/article/quality-101-identifying-the-core-components-of-a-high-quality-early-childhood-program/

World Health Organization (2005). The effects of air pollution on children's health and development: A review of the evidence. http://www.euro.who.int/document/E86575.pdf.

Worsley, T. D., & Roby, R. S. (2021). Fostering spaces for Black joy in STEM-rich making and beyond. *Journal of Effective Teaching in Higher Education, 4*(2), 118–134. https://doi.org/10.36021/jethe.v4i2.166

Wyse, R., Hwang, W. T., Ahmed, A. A., et al. (2020). Diversity by race, ethnicity, and sex within the US psychiatry physician workforce. *Academic Psychiatry, 44*(5), 523–530. https://doi.org/10.1007/s40596-020-01276-z

Xu, J., Kochanek, K. D., Murphy, S. L., et al. (2014). Mortality in the United States, 2012 (No. 168). US Department of Health and Human Services, Centers for Disease Control and Prevention, National Center for Health Statistics. https://pubmed.ncbi.nlm.nih.gov/26727391/

Yang, W., Huang, R., Su, Y., et al. (2022). Coaching early childhood teachers: A systematic review of its effects on teacher instruction and child development. *Review of Education, 10*(1), e3343. https://doi.org/10.1002/rev3.3343

Yearby, R. (2021). Reifying racism in the COVID-19 pandemic response. *The American Journal of Bioethics, 21*(3), 75–78. https://doi.org/10.1080/15265161.2020.1870773

Yosso, T. J. (2005). Whose culture has capital? A critical race theory discussion of community cultural wealth. *Race Ethnicity and Education*, *8*(1), 69–91. https://doi.org/10.1080/1361332052000341006

Zahner, G. E., & Daskalakis, C. (1997). Factors associated with mental health, general health, and school-based service use for child psychopathology. *American Journal of Public Health*, *87*(9), 1440–1448. https://doi.org/10.2105/ajph.87.9.1440

Zeger, S. L., Dominici, F., McDermott, A., et al. (2008). Mortality in the Medicare population and chronic exposure to fine particulate air pollution in urban centers (2000–2005). *Environmental Health Perspectives*, *116*(12), 1614–1619. https://doi.org/10.1289/ehp.11449

Zero to Three (2023). Infant and early childhood mental health. www.thinkbabies .org/policy-priorities-infant-and-early-childhood-mental-health/?_ga= 2.89418264.2081815665.1671216472-1723127281.1671216472

Zippel, C. (2021). 9 in 10 families with low incomes are using child tax credits to pay for necessities and education. Center on Budget and Policy Priorities. www.cbpp.org/blog/9-in-10-families-with-low-incomes-are-using-child-tax-credits-to-pay-for-necessities-education

Zoch, J., M., Hopkins, E. J., Jensen, H., et al. (2017, November). Learning through play: A review of the evidence. The Lego Foundation. https://cms .learningthroughplay.com/media/wmtlmbe0/learning-through-play_web.pdf

Cambridge Elements ≡

Child Development

Marc H. Bornstein

National Institute of Child Health and Human Development, Bethesda

Institute for Fiscal Studies, London

UNICEF, New York City

Marc H. Bornstein is an Affiliate of the Eunice Kennedy Shriver National Institute of Child Health and Human Development, an International Research Fellow at the Institute for Fiscal Studies (London), and UNICEF Senior Advisor for Research for ECD Parenting Programmes. Bornstein is President Emeritus of the Society for Research in Child Development, Editor Emeritus of *Child Development*, and founding Editor of *Parenting: Science and Practice*.

About the Series

Child development is a lively and engaging, yet serious and real-world subject of scientific study that encompasses myriad theories, methods, substantive areas, and applied concerns. Cambridge Elements in Child Development addresses many contemporary topics in child development with unique, comprehensive, and state-of-the-art treatments of principal issues, primary currents of thinking, original perspectives, and empirical contributions to understanding early human development.

Cambridge Elements ≡

Child Development

Elements in the Series